# Answered
## PRAYER
*Guaranteed!*

# Answered
# PRAYER
## *Guaranteed!*

# Frederick K. C. Price

CHARISMA
**HOUSE**

Most CHARISMA HOUSE BOOK GROUP products are available at special quantity discounts for bulk purchase for sales promotions, premiums, fund-raising, and educational needs. For details, write Charisma House Book Group, 600 Rinehart Road, Lake Mary, Florida 32746, or telephone (407) 333-0600.

ANSWERED PRAYER GUARANTEED! by Frederick K. C. Price
Published by Charisma House
Charisma Media/Charisma House Book Group
600 Rinehart Road, Lake Mary, Florida 32746
www.charismahouse.com

Unless otherwise noted, all Scripture quotations are from the New King James Version of the Bible. Copyright © 1979, 1980, 1982 by Thomas Nelson, Inc., publishers. Used by permission.

Scripture quotations marked AMP are from the Amplified Bible. Old Testament copyright © 1965, 1987 by the Zondervan Corporation. The Amplified New Testament copyright © 1954, 1958, 1987 by the Lockman Foundation. Used by permission.

Scripture quotations marked ASV are from the American Standard Bible.

Scripture quotations from the Worrell New Testament are in public domain.

Cover design by Justin Evans; Design Director: Bill Johnson

Visit the author's website at www.faithdome.org.

International Standard Book Number: 978-1-61638-490-6

The Library of Congress has catalogued the previous edition as follows:

**Library of Congress Cataloging-in-Publication Data:**
Price, Frederick K. C.
  Answered prayer-- guaranteed! / Frederick K.C. Price. -- 1st ed.
     p. cm.
  ISBN 1-59979-012-2 (hard back)
  1. Prayer--Christianity.  I. Title.
  BV220.P75 2006
  248.3'2--dc22
                                    2006010443

E-book ISBN: 978-1-59979-701-4

21 22 23 24 25 — 9 8 7 6 5
Printed in the United States of America

# ACKNOWLEDGMENTS

First, I would like to thank my heavenly Father; my Savior and Lord Jesus Christ, the head of the church; and the Holy Spirit, who is the one who has enlightened me and revealed to me the truths as to how to pray and be guaranteed to receive the answer to all of my prayers, so that I could share these principles with others.

Of course, a book like this takes team effort, and I would like to take this time to acknowledge and thank those who helped to make it happen. It is not my desire to leave anyone out, so if I fail to mention your name, please know that it was not my intent. And I thank you from the bottom of my heart for whatever part you had to play in making this book a reality.

Professor Larry Schweikart of the University of Dayton (Ohio) served as my chief editor, and I thank him for his tireless and efficient work. I would like to thank Cynthia King of UD for her proofreading help.

I'd like to thank Marcus Andrews for helping me to realize that I needed to write a book on prayer. I want to thank my daughter Angela Evans for acting as my "agent" to bring my authorship to Stephen Strang's attention.

I'd like to thank Stephen Strang of Charisma Media (formerly Strang Communications) for his willingness to publish this book and for his foresight in recognizing the value that the contents of my book bring to the body of Christ. A special thank you to Bert Ghezzi, former editorial director for Charisma House, for his insight and influence in recommending this book to Stephen Strang.

Thank you to Barbara Dycus for her editing work.

Thanks to Michelle McIntosh, publications coordinator for Faith One Publishing, for her efforts on behalf of this book and to Doris Pettigrew, our transcriber.

Thanks to my attorney, John D. Diamond, for his excellent negotiating skills and knowledge of book publishing.

To the congregation of Crenshaw Christian Center and the loyal viewers of *Ever Increasing Faith Ministries*, I say thank you for your support through the years.

And lastly, I cannot forget my wife, Betty, and our children: Angela and her husband, Michael Evans; Cheryl Price; Stephanie and her husband, Danon Buchanan; and Frederick and his wife, Angel Price. Their support has been extremely important and valuable to me over the years.

# Contents

# Contents

# INTRODUCTION

How do you pray?

"Well, I get down on my knees or go into my room and…"

Wait, that's not what I meant. I mean, what method, what process do you use to pray? Are your prayers answered? How do you know?

There is a popular saying among pastors today that states, "God answers all prayers, but sometimes God says yes, sometimes God says no, and sometimes God says wait." Doesn't that seem like an odd form of answer to you? I mean, if you order a Big Mac at McDonald's and you pay your money, you expect a hamburger. Barring the extremely unusual situation that McDonald's runs out of meat or french fries, once you pay your money, no isn't an option, and, for most people, wait isn't an option either.

Is it true that *no* and *wait* are God's answers to prayer? If not, are you getting what you pray for? And if you do not get what you pray for, why not?

Next to the salvation experience and receiving the Holy Spirit, there is no issue in all of a Christian's spiritual life that is as critical as *getting prayer right!* Yet you'd be amazed at how many people don't know that not only are there different kinds of prayers, but also that you can no more use the wrong prayer to get a certain result than you can use a Phillips head screwdriver when you need a hammer. Prayer permeates a Christian's life. It should be the first thing a Christian does in the morning, and it should be, as Paul commanded, done "without ceasing" during the day.

Unfortunately, most Christians are not informed that there are different types of prayer and that there is a proper *formula* for praying, so they attempt to use flowery language capped by a catch-all phrase, "If it be Thy will." People who do this are well meaning. They are sincere. But usually they are sincerely wrong, and they rarely get prayers answered.

Other people, like a desperate quarterback at the end of a football game, just "throw a prayer up there" and hope it sticks. They hope that whatever they ask, and however they ask it, God will respond. But will He? Is God obligated to act if we don't follow the rules?

This book is a formula for answered prayer—how to do prayer. Have you ever said, "I hope God heard that prayer"? Would you like to be assured that if you follow His instructions you can be guaranteed He will hear you every time? In the following pages, I want to share with you one of the biggest blessings of my life: *God's instruction manual for prayer*. This is not some gimmick. Don't think for a moment you are treating God like a supernatural *candy dispenser*. Quite the contrary, the principles I am going to share with you involve taking God at His Word. They require that we "put up or shut up" with our faith. That's why some people resist what I'm about to tell you, because it's all about faith—faith, and knowing God's promises.

There is a way to pray so that you know God hears you and has already answered your prayer. There is a way to pray in faith—all the time—a way to get answers.

And no isn't an answer.

# CHAPTER ONE

# USE THE RIGHT TOOL

*Many Christians aren't aware that there
are several different types of prayer discussed
in the Bible, and if you use the rules or
tools from one prayer when you should be
using the tools from another prayer for your
needs or your requests, it won't work.*

Have you ever watched a talented mechanic or crafts-man work? He always has the right tool. You or I might strain to reach underneath an engine or struggle with pliers to put together some little piece of furniture. But for a master mechanic or trained craftsman, it seems that no problem is too great. The mechanic whips out a long instrument that has a ratchet on the end, slithers it up through the crowded engine compartment, and has a bolt out in seconds. A craftsman can affix the perfect-sized screwdriver head to an electric drill and assemble a complex-looking bookcase in minutes. If you talk to these people, they will always tell you that it is critical to use the right tool. A screw won't come off easily with pliers—if at all, and you can't drive in a nail with a screwdriver.

5

This principle is critical when it comes to prayer. Many Christians aren't aware that there are several different types of prayer discussed in the Bible, and if you use the *rules* or *tools* from one prayer when you should be using the tools from another prayer for your needs or your request, it won't work. You would be applying the wrong spiritual tool to your needs or your request. Consider what Paul wrote to the Ephesians. He concludes a long section in which he urges the Christians at Ephesus to "put on the whole armor of God" (Eph. 6:11), then to "stand" (v. 14), saying this should be done by "praying always with all prayer and supplication in the Spirit" (v. 18). I'll deal later with the concept of "praying always," but notice that Paul tells us to pray with "all prayer." This refers to all kinds of prayer, or to put it in a different way, Paul is saying there are different kinds of prayer.

---

*How to pray* and *what to pray for*
are entirely different issues.

---

A failure to understand that there are different kinds of prayer and that they don't all do the same thing has led some ministers to claim we cannot pray correctly at all, or to conclude each prayer with "if it be Thy will." They frequently use Romans 8:26 as a proof text to show that we do not know what we need, so, in essence, we can't possibly pray correctly:

> Likewise the Spirit also helps in our weaknesses. For we
> do not know what we should pray for as we ought, but
> the Spirit Himself makes intercession for us with groan-
> ings which cannot be uttered.
>
> —Romans 8:26

Let me note in passing that this passage is sometimes used by ministers to claim that we don't know what we should pray for. Yet these same ministers may deny praying in tongues, which seems clearly indicated by this verse. We will discuss this more in a later chapter.

*How to pray* and *what to pray for* are entirely different issues. Can we agree on that? What I use my car for and how to start it have little to do with each other. This verse does not say that we do not know *how* to pray. It says we do not know *"what we should pray for as we ought"* (emphasis added).

The context of this verse deals with intercession for others. Paul was discussing *intercessory prayer*, which is a totally differ-ent type of prayer tool than what we call *petition prayer*.

It helps to know from the outset what the different prayer tools are—to know a ratchet from a screwdriver, as it were, in the realm of prayer. We have no problem understanding that baseball, basketball, and soccer all have different types of balls, different playing surfaces, and different rules. Why is it so hard to think that prayer is any different? In fact, there are six differ-ent types of prayer mentioned in the Bible, and God intended them for different functions.

## 1. The Prayer of Agreement

In Matthew 18:19, Jesus introduced *the prayer of agreement* when He said:

> Again I say to you that if two of you agree on earth concerning anything that they ask, it will be done for them by My Father in heaven.

Right off the bat you can see that for the prayer of agreement to work, people involved in the prayer have to...*agree*! You cannot know what someone else wants—what someone is believing for—and God cannot answer your prayer for someone else against his or her will. To use the prayer of agreement, you must be sure that the person with whom you are agreeing is in line with what you are asking for. If someone asks me to pray in agreement with them, I ask, "What specifically do you want me to pray for?" Even husbands and wives sometimes are not in agreement over what to pray for when they use the prayer of agreement. If they are praying for a new car, the husband might be praying for a sports car, while the wife is praying for a small SUV. Neither of them can get their prayer answered because they are not really in agreement.

You absolutely must be on the same page when using the prayer of agreement. It is even difficult to set yourself in agreement with people over their healing, because often *healing* to you may mean something totally different than what *healing* means to a sick person. Some sick people just want to be out of pain. A person may be praying for a doctor to provide a cure—and there is nothing wrong with that, *unless* you are praying for the person's supernatural healing. It isn't the same thing! As a pastor, I have even had people ask me to pray for them to be well when in actuality they were believing to *die*. One time, after I had just started out in faith as a minister, a young woman who was sick seemed to be getting worse and worse. Finally I asked this woman, "What are you praying for? I'm praying for your healing."

---

> To use the prayer of agreement, you must be sure that the person with whom you are agreeing is in line with what you are asking for.

---

She replied that she wanted to die—that she'd been in an abusive marriage and that she was just as happy to go and be with the Lord as to continue living with her husband. So here I was, praying for her to live, and she was praying to die!

In that situation, whose prayer do you think will take precedence with God? It would be hers, because we cannot violate her free will, nor can God. Get some information before you commit yourself in prayer agreement with someone else. If you are both in complete agreement, then watch out! You will have double the faith working on a problem.

I want to reiterate, though, that you cannot use the prayer of faith or the prayer of consecration and dedication if you need the prayer of agreement. Use the right tool. The prayer of agreement is useful in the context of marriages, say, when a husband and wife are buying a new home and need guidance on which home to buy. Or the prayer of agreement works quite well in a business setting where two Christians are in business together and are believing for a specific sales target. Make sure you are in perfect agreement about what your prayer request is before you join with another believer in the prayer of agreement.

## 2. THE PRAYER OF FAITH

The prayer of faith, also known as petition prayer, is the prayer that most people think of when they use the term *prayer*. Petition prayer is between you and God. It is you asking God for a particular outcome, whether it's a job, money, a lifetime mate, or whatever. The key verse for the prayer of faith is Mark 11:24, where Jesus says:

> Therefore I say to you, whatever things you ask when you pray, believe that you receive them, and you will have them.

The rule to consider here is *when you pray*—not after you pray...not when you feel something...not when you see something. *When you pray* (the moment that you pray) you must believe that you receive what you asked for.

This is a difficult concept for some people. God is a present tense God. He doesn't operate in the past or in the future, but in the *now*. Whenever you pray, at that moment you are in the present. At that precise time, you must believe that you receive what you are praying for. At the moment you pray, believe that you receive what you have requested. Hebrews 11:1 says, "Now faith is the substance of things hoped for, the evidence of things not seen." Your faith is *substance*—it is something real, something tangible. It is evidence of things you cannot see.

Think of a court of law. The jury was not at the scene of a crime, but the attorney introduces a photo of the crime scene that shows blood. That photo takes the place of the "thing" itself, the crime scene. The evidence is proof of something the juror cannot see but knows nonetheless. Your faith is proof of something that you have received…but can't yet see. The Amplified Bible says it this way: "Now faith is the assurance (the confirmation, the title deed) of the things [we] hope for, being the proof of things [we] do not see and the conviction of their reality [faith perceiving as real fact what is not revealed to the senses]." The Worrell New Testament says, "Now faith is an assurance of things hoped for, a sure persuasion of things not seen." Confirmation. Title deed. Assurance. Sure persuasion. Substance. It doesn't get any clearer than that.

---

**If you have asked God for something
once, you must have faith enough
to believe that He heard you and
that He has answered your prayer.**

---

Notice that Mark 11:24 does not say when you will actually *see* the result of your prayer. It does not tell you how long it will take for that prayer result to appear, and this is where many Christians get hung up. God lives in one eternal now. There is no past or present for Him. But we are temporal beings who live in the context of time. When you pray in faith, God immediately gives you what you prayed for—in the spirit realm. But in the natural world, due to a number of factors, it may take time for the answer to manifest itself. As an example, when you make a stock market transaction and tell your broker to sell one hundred dollars of stock, he sells it right then. But you do not possess the actual money until he sends it to you through the mail or transmits it electronically to your account. Even then, you will likely get a check, and that check does you no good until you endorse it and put it in your account. We do not have a problem understanding these processes we have to go through in the natural world. We know they are required to bring something you *have* into a reality you can use.

Let me give you yet another example. You may get your new credit card in the mail with instructions from the bank that you must make a phone call to activate the card. That card is in your name, and it has a limit of many thousand dollars set aside for you—yet it will not work unless you go through the right steps to activate that card.

Part of the faith required to make a prayer *transaction*, to *activate* your faith request, is that you can only pray *one time* for something—because if you believe you have already received it, why would you ask for it again? Imagine I'm standing in front of you, and I say, "Please give me your Bible."

You reach down, pull out your Bible, and hand it to me.

Then I say, "Please give me your Bible."

What? You would rightly say, "Are you crazy? I just gave you my Bible." If you have asked God for something once, you must have faith enough to believe that He heard you and that He has answered your prayer. That's what Jesus meant when He said, "Believe that you receive them" (referring to things you prayed for).

God answers prayers, and He will answer your specific prayer in line with His Word (more on that later), *but* it is your faith that brings that answer out of the spiritual world and into the physical world. How many times in Scripture does Jesus say to someone, "According to your faith...," or "Daughter, your faith has made you whole"? He referred to peoples' faith constantly, and even though it was His power that healed them, He always credited their faith with being the catalyst. In fact, when Jesus went to His hometown, we are told: "Now He did not do many mighty works there because of their unbelief" (Matt. 13:58). Well, I have a question for you: Did Jesus suddenly lose His power on that visit to Nazareth? Was there some satanic kryptonite that stole His powers? Did He suddenly cease being the Son of God? No! His power never changed. What changed? It was the people's level of faith mixed with His power.

There is a simple spiritual explanation for this. God will not do something against your will. God cannot violate free will. If you don't have faith to do something, He won't violate your will. In this case, He won't arbitrarily override your lack of faith. When blind men came to Jesus and asked that He restore their sight, He asked them, "Do you believe that I am able to do this?" (Matt. 9:28). They said, "Yes," and He said, "According to your faith let it be to you" (v. 29). The Bible actually indicates that they *received* their sight. Just as the air you breathe is already there—but you must inhale it, so their healing was already there, and they had to take it by faith.

---

**Don't think your request is an affront to God. If He has provided for it and promised it, you are fully within the rights He has given you to ask for it.**

---

So what should you pray for? The answer to that question is simple: you pray for those things that God promises to you in the Bible. "Does that mean cars? They didn't have cars in Jesus's time. How could I pray for that?"

Maybe some technologies, specifically, did not exist in the past, but that doesn't mean that the concept isn't in the Bible. Cars serve a purpose—to transport us from one place to another, to make our lives easier. So do houses, and so do bank accounts. They all fall under the rubric of prosperity or wealth. A better question would be, "Does God promise me prosperity?" Yes, He does.

Many—though certainly not all—of God's promises are outlined in a tremendous chapter in the Book of Deuteronomy, chapter 28, where God tells the children of Israel that if they "hear and obey" God's Word, He will bless them. Just look at a few of the promises God makes in chapter 28:

> Blessed shall you be in the city, and blessed shall you be in the country. Blessed shall be the fruit of your body, the produce of your ground and the increase of your herds, the increase of your cattle and the offspring of your flocks. Blessed shall be your basket and your kneading bowl. Blessed shall you be when you come in, and blessed shall you be when you go out. The LORD will cause your enemies who rise against you to be defeated before your face; they shall come out against you one way and flee before you seven ways. The LORD will command the blessing on you in your storehouses and in all to which you set your hand, and He will bless you in the land which the LORD your God is giving you.
>
> —DEUTERONOMY 28:3–8

Now, while cars are not specifically mentioned, it seems pretty clear that if you are blessed in the above manner, you'll be able to buy any car you want. Certainly "herds" could have referred as easily to horses as to, more likely, cattle. If we Christians are indeed the "seed of Abraham," as Paul says, then we are promised prosperity. So you can either pray for a car or pray for the money to buy a car—either way it has been promised to you. And God doesn't care if you have a Volkswagen or a Ferrari or a Ford. They are all the same to God. (He has

15

heavenly chariots!) Some Christians can't really believe for the car they want because they feel unworthy or guilty asking for something that is very expensive. God does not care about the expense. He lives in the most luxurious, wealthy city to ever exist. Our earthly concepts of wealth are dwarfed by His riches—and I don't mean just spiritual riches. Don't think your request is an affront to God. If He has provided for it and promised it, you are fully within the rights He has given you to ask for it.

However, even if you are praying a petition prayer—the prayer of faith—in the context of agreeing with someone else, it will not work if, again, you are not in complete agreement. Your faith cannot override the faith of another person.

## 3. THE PRAYER OF CONSECRATION AND DEDICATION

In Luke 22:41–42, we see outlined the *prayer of consecration and dedication:*

> And He [Jesus] was withdrawn from them [Peter, James, and John] about a stone's throw, and He knelt down and prayed, saying, "Father, if it is Your will, take this cup away from Me; nevertheless not My will, but Yours, be done."

Jesus knew that God was the Creator and Ruler of the universe. If there was any way man's salvation could be accomplished, God would know how to do it. Jesus was looking at separation from the Father for the first time ever—not just in His earthly life but through all eternity. He was praying, in essence, "If there is any other way to do this, let's do it that way." But the key for Jesus, and for us, is, "Nevertheless not My will, but Yours, be done." You pray that God's will be done only when you don't know that will or do not know if an alternative path that appears is equally "correct" or godly.

---

## Sometimes we want our Jordans to be cut off before we get there, but that's not faith.

---

I was ministering in a denominational church when God began to deal with me about leaving that church and starting an independent ministry. But even though I was certain God was telling me to leave, He didn't give me explicit instructions on where to go. In other words, God didn't say, "Frederick, thou shalt go to Hollywood and startest thy ministry there," or "Frederick, take thyself and thy family to Compton, and there shalt thou teach." (Actually, God doesn't speak in King James English to modern Americans, but I just used that for effect.) Like Abraham, I had some marching orders but no specific direction. So I prayed the prayer of consecration and dedication: "Father, if it is Your will that I go to Los Angeles to start a church, I'm willing to go to Los Angeles; but if it's Your will that I go to Santa Monica, then I will go there."

In the absence of direct instructions, the prayer of consecration and dedication says you will allow God to set your direction or make your decisions. You might say, "Shouldn't God be making all my decisions?" No! You don't want to make all your children's decisions for them. They must learn to decide things on their own, but you hope that they make the right decisions out of the full spectrum of options they have. God doesn't want to control us like puppets—He wants us to be mature Christians capable of making the kinds of decisions Jesus would make if it were up to Jesus.

The prayer of consecration and dedication works when you have two (or more) godly alternatives before you, and you are not getting a clear sense at that time of which road, as it were, God wants you to take. Yogi Berra once said that he came to a fork in the road and took it! Well, when the direction is unclear—but any of the options appear to be legitimate, righteous options—that is the perfect time to say, "Lord, if it be Your will, I'm going to go with Option A." Believe me, He will let you know if you are taking the wrong fork in the road. Just think about Abraham—he had no idea where he was going. We don't have a lot of information about his journey, but you know there had to have been times where one pass ran over a mountain and another across a river, and Abraham had to say, "Lord, which direction should I go? Your will be done."

When I started Crenshaw Christian Center, God did not show me the whole picture. He doesn't show us the whole picture because it would not take any faith then—all you would have to do is follow the map. When Joshua led the children of Israel across the Jordan, God instructed them that the priests bearing the ark of the covenant should "stand in the Jordan"

(Josh. 3:7–8). Joshua then passed on the words of the Lord: "And it shall come to pass, as soon as the soles of the feet of the priests who bear the ark of the LORD, the Lord of all the earth, shall rest in the waters of the Jordan, that the waters of the Jordan shall be cut off, the waters that come down from upstream" (v. 13). Notice that they had to actually get in the water before God did anything about the water. Sometimes we want our Jordans to be cut off before we get there, but that's not faith.

So, to review, when you pray a prayer of consecration and dedication, you would always use the phrase "If it be Your will." But if you are praying a petition prayer or prayer of faith, you *never* use "If it be Your will," because that would be saying to God that you do not know what God's will is for you. That is why you must know what God has promised you, whether it's healing, prosperity, or whatever, and not be in the dark.

## 4. THE PRAYER OF PRAISE AND WORSHIP

In this prayer, you are not asking God to do something for you or to give you something. You are not even asking for direction and dedicating your life to whatever it is God has called you to do. Rather, you just want to praise the Lord, to thank Him for His many blessings and mercy. You want to tell Him how much you love Him. A good example of this type of prayer appears in Luke 2:20, discussing the reaction of the shepherds who had seen the baby Jesus:

19

> Then the shepherds returned, glorifying and praising
> God for all the things they had heard and seen, as it
> was told them.

This means that it happened just as the angel of the Lord said it would. In Luke 18:43, we see the blind man "glorifying God. And all the people, when they saw it, gave praise to God." Ostensibly, they prayed prayers of thanksgiving.

Look at how Jesus prayed in John 11:41: "Father, I thank You that You have heard Me," referring to His previous prayer regarding Lazarus. In the Lord's Prayer, which I will discuss at length later, Jesus told His disciples: "When you pray, say: Our Father in heaven, hallowed be Your name" (Luke 11:2). Paul wrote to the Philippians: "Be anxious for nothing, but in everything by prayer and supplication, with thanksgiving, let your requests be made known to God" (Phil. 4:6). This says that even when we pray the prayer of faith, we should always intersperse worship and praise.

The prayer of praise and worship is the only prayer that you are permitted to direct to *Jesus* rather than the Father. It is perfectly acceptable to say, "Thank You, Jesus, for Your love, Your sacrifice, Your obedience, and Your perfection. Thank You for saving me." In John 15:16, Jesus said, "You did not choose Me, but I chose you and appointed you that you should go and bear fruit, and that your fruit should remain, that whatever you ask the Father *in My name* He may give you" (emphasis added). All petition prayers are to be directed to "the Father, in My [i.e., Jesus's] name." No exceptions!

In the prayer of consecration and dedication, you are asking God for His direction—not Jesus. But in the prayer of praise and worship, you are free to address the Son directly and thank Him for His sacrifice, His courage, His consistency, His mercy, and His love. Praise the Lord at every opportunity.

## 5. THE PRAYER OF INTERCESSION

Intercession means you are interceding—acting in prayer—on behalf of someone else. This person may be incapable of praying for himself or herself. Perhaps the person is on drugs or mentally confused by demonic doctrines. Perhaps the person is so sick he or she can't muster the energy to stay awake, let alone pray. On a general level, intercession involves praying in a general sense for others. For example: "Father, bless and protect our troops overseas in the war zone that they would return home to their families." You aren't identifying a particular individual or even a particular unit. In general intercessory prayer, you pray, for example, for the church or for our government.

In Ephesians 1:15–18, Paul wrote:

> Therefore I also, after I heard of your faith in the Lord Jesus and your love for all the saints, do not cease to give thanks for you, making mention of you in my prayers; that the God of our Lord Jesus Christ, the Father of glory, may give to you the spirit of wisdom and revelation in the knowledge of Him, the eyes of your understanding being enlightened; that you may know what is the hope of His calling, what are the riches of the glory of His inheritance in the saints.

21

This goes on, but Paul is making it plain that he prays for the church at Ephesus and for the individuals there to receive these blessings. He does not set himself in agreement with anyone, so this seems to be a good example of intercessory prayer. Likewise, in his greeting to the Philippians, he wrote: "I thank my God upon every remembrance of you, always in every prayer of mine making request for you all with joy" (Phil. 1:3–4). The fact that Paul said he made requests *for* them suggests that this also was an intercessory prayer.

### The role of the Holy Spirit in intercessory prayer

However, in Romans 8:26, Paul presents a different type of intercessory prayer—a higher kind of intercessory prayer: "Likewise the Spirit also helps our weaknesses. For we do not know what we should pray for as we ought, but the Spirit Himself makes intercession for us with groanings which cannot be uttered." This verse gets into the whole issue of being filled with the Holy Spirit, which is why the devil resists this kind of prayer so much. In order to explain this we will take a brief detour from our analysis of the different types of prayer.

---

When a burden of intercession is placed on you, you need to pray right then. The Holy Spirit has plans for you to be a conduit to help or bless someone else.

---

People have the idea that God can do *anything*. In a sense, yes, He can, but in the truest legal sense, no, He may not. God has the *power* to do whatever He wants, but He has structured the system to work by laws—natural laws and spiritual laws, which involve spiritual authority. As the One who gave the law, He cannot Himself break the laws. Psalm 138:1–2 tells us: "I will praise You with my whole heart.... For You have magnified Your word above all Your name." In other words, God's Word—His laws—are more important than even His name, because if He doesn't observe His own Word, then He is no different than we are.

Moreover, God cannot and will not trespass on someone else's will. When He gave the earth to Adam, Adam literally became the "god of this world." He was the man; he was in charge. But in the Fall, Adam handed this over to Satan. In a legal sense, he gave Satan the title deed to Planet Earth. Satan was the new owner. Technically, the earth became the devil's property, and God cannot *legally* trespass on this earth without permission. I own a house—it's my house. I have the title deed. I can invite whomever I want into my house for a party, and as long as we don't disturb the peace—and you know how wild we ministers of the gospel can get!—no one can say anything about whom I let into my house.

This house—the earth—was made for man. We have a right to be here, or, more appropriately, *had* a right to be here until Satan bamboozled Adam and got the title deed. Jesus Christ bought this back with His blood, but the purchase had a lease clause wherein the devil still maintained legal control

23

until the last days, when Jesus would evict him. I can give you an example of this from personal experience with our Pepperdine property. We had some undesirable tenants who had promised to leave. Still, we could not get them out—even though we owned that property—until that lease was up because they had a legal right to be there.

This explains why Hurricane Katrina, the tsunami in Asia, and the earthquakes in Pakistan were not "acts of God" but rather acts of the devil. *He* is the one still legally in charge of this planet. He has the lease. It is his domain. You may ask, "Dr. Price, do you mean to say that God isn't more powerful than the devil?"

No! That isn't what I mean. In the twinkling of an eye, God could flush that old liar into the eternal pit of fire. But God *cannot* violate His word, and He gave His word to Adam that he would have dominion over the earth. Dominion means you have authority and control. Remember that if you can't sell something or give it away, you really don't have dominion over it. Through sin, Adam gave up his dominion over the earth to the devil. Therefore, God cannot legally violate the devil's *civil rights* when it comes to authority over this world.

---

*For a temptation to be real, you must be able to yield to it.* Otherwise it is little more than an invalid offer.

---

24

Jesus said in John 14:30, "I will no longer talk much with you, for the ruler of this world is coming, and he has nothing in Me." Jesus the Christ called the devil "the ruler of this world." Not God, but Satan. The word *ruler* in the New King James Bible is translated "prince" in the King James Version. In Greek, the word for "prince" is *archon*, meaning "ruler."

In Luke 4:5–8 the devil makes an offer to Jesus:

> Then the devil, taking Him up on a high mountain, showed Him all the kingdoms of the world in a moment of time. And the devil said to Him, "All this authority I will give You, and their glory; for *this has been delivered to me* and I give it to whomever I wish. Therefore, if You will worship before me, all will be Yours." And Jesus answered and said to him, "Get behind Me, Satan! For it is written, 'You shall worship the LORD your God, and Him only you shall serve.'"
>
> —EMPHASIS ADDED

Notice something very important here. Jesus did not say to the devil, "You liar! You don't own these kingdoms, and they aren't yours to give!" Jesus could not say that, because Satan, for once in his mangy life, was telling the truth. Those kingdoms—the entire earth—had indeed been "delivered" to him with a big red bow from Adam. And it was just as true that the devil could have given them to "whomever I wish." (If you don't own something, you can't give it away.)

There is still more to this verse, though, that makes it clear that the devil had dominion over this world. Have you ever heard the word *temptation*? What is the purpose of temptation?

It is to get you to yield to the temptation, correct? I submit to you that if you cannot yield to temptation, it is not a temptation. Arab princes castrated slaves and made them into eunuchs so that they would not be tempted to have sex with the women in the harems. Let me give you a somewhat different example. If you offered me $10 billion to get pregnant, that would be no temptation to me whatsoever. Why? Because it's physically impossible for me to get pregnant. It would be like offering someone whatever they wanted if they could flap their wings and fly off a cliff. It won't happen.

*For a temptation to be real, you must be able to yield to it.* Otherwise it is little more than an invalid offer. Let's look back to our verses in Luke. Jesus could not have been tempted by the devil's offer if in fact the devil did not have legal title to all the kingdoms he showed Jesus. Luke 4:6 states: "And the devil said to Him, 'All this authority I will give you, and their glory; for it has been delivered to me.'" He didn't even say he bought it—Satan said it was "delivered to me, and I give it to whomever I wish." If the devil was lying, Jesus would have had to clarify this immediately for our benefit and challenge him—but He never did because it was true. It *was* a temptation, because the earth belonged to the devil, and he could, indeed, offer it to Jesus.

### The role of the believer

At this point, you might say, "What's the use? If God cannot do anything, aren't we doomed?" I didn't say God can't do anything—but He can only do those things in this earth realm that His Word, His promises, and His law allow Him to do. That's where we come in. God's will is that no one die in sin. "For God so loved the world that He gave His only begotten Son, that whoever believes in Him should not perish but have everlasting life" (John 3:16). There is a qualifier in that promise: "whoever believes." Before God can save you (according to His own Word, His own rules, and His own promises), you must *believe*.

"Do you mean to tell me that God cannot save whomever He wants?"

That's right. God cannot and will not save you against your will. Likewise, He cannot and will not force you to accept the Holy Spirit or to speak in tongues. He will not send you on a mission trip you do not want to go on. God can encourage you; He can inspire you; He can set up circumstances to guide you; but He will not *force* you to act against your will.

Hollywood makes many movies, and most of them are not worth watching, but every once in a while the producers and directors—perhaps unintentionally and perhaps even guided quietly by God—end up making some movies that have a powerful spiritual message. In 2003 there was a movie called *Bruce Almighty*, with Jim Carrey as "Bruce," a television features reporter, and Morgan Freeman as "God." The plot centered on Bruce thinking God no longer cared about him, or anyone, and whining that he, Bruce, could do a better job running the universe. So, the movie depicted God handing over some of His power and letting Bruce try it. Not only did Bruce discover that having unlimited power doesn't produce happiness, but he also found that merely granting people every wish they want is a disaster. (The hidden message here is that the power of God must be used within the guidelines instituted by God.)

Perhaps the most spiritual gem in that movie came when Bruce, who is in love with the appropriately named "Grace" (who continually forgives Bruce for his self-centered behavior), finally drives her off. He asks God, "How do you make somebody love you without affecting free will?"

---

One of the devices the devil uses
to prevent people from praying in
the Spirit is this: "You don't know
what you're saying." That's right,
you don't. You have to trust God.

---

God laughs and says, "Welcome to My world, son." You see, that is indeed the difficulty of allowing us puny humans to have free will—once God gave us that great and awesome responsibility, He could not take it back without violating His own Word. Love—and obedience—must be freely given, not commanded.

God has set up the system, and it still works *if we work it.* In Matthew 9:38, the Lord Jesus Christ Himself said, "Therefore pray the Lord of the harvest to send out laborers into His harvest." Jesus told His disciples to "pray...to send out laborers." It is *God's* harvest—but *we* are responsible for bringing it in. We are the only ones who have legal right to act on

28

Satan's ground, on his property. We can invite in whomever we want, and in our case, that would be God. Once we invite Him in, the devil can't do anything—free will, remember? It works both ways.

That is where intercession comes in. We need to be praying for one another. If you know a specific need—Susie needs a job, or Charles is going in for surgery—then you can intercede for that person specifically over that issue. However, most times we do not know all the circumstances of other people, and as a result, we might not be helping them that much. For example, Susie may think she needs a job, but her real problem is that even though her husband makes plenty of money, she spends twice that amount. Maybe her real issue is overspending and an undisciplined financial life, not insufficient income. Maybe Charles appears to need pancreas surgery—but his real problem is a tumor that neither he nor you, or even the doctors, know about yet. That is why the truest form of prayer—the highest level—is mentioned in Romans 8:26. This is the purest form of intercessory prayer:

> Likewise the Spirit also helps in our weaknesses. For we do not know what we should pray for as we ought, but the Spirit Himself makes intercession for us with groanings which cannot be uttered.

When a burden of intercession is placed on you (I use the term *burden* not as something negative but only an awareness), you need to pray right then. The Holy Spirit has plans for you to be a conduit to help or bless someone else.

**The Spirit and the believer working together**

Yet the verse says you don't know what you are praying for, correct? This is where the rubber meets the road and where we end up with a lot of resistance. No, in the natural, you do not know what you are praying for, unless by the word of knowledge the Holy Spirit has made you aware that Susie is spending too much or that Charles has a tumor. This is the purpose of praying in tongues.

---

## Intercessory prayer can only work if it is in line with God's plans and His law.

---

In "normal" prayer—when you pray in English—your thoughts, prejudices, and fears can intervene and mess things up. Have you ever started to pray for someone, then suddenly had an unkind thought about, perhaps, how that person treated you once? Likewise, in "normal" prayer in English, you can be easily distracted because you are organizing the prayer in your mind. How many times have you started to pray and the phone would ring? Or the dog needs to go out? Or any number of other things take you off stride? Moreover, even if we are not diverted, we have trouble praying a *pure* prayer that is not infested with our own hang-ups. You want Tammy to have that job, but you know if she gets it that she will be your boss, and that might be uncomfortable.

The Holy Spirit will give our own spirit the information to pray about, and we will pray pure and unadulterated prayer in the Spirit, that is, in other tongues. We do not have to know what we are praying about! One of the devices the devil uses to prevent people from praying in the Spirit is this: "You don't know what you're saying." That's right, you don't. You have to trust God. What are you really concerned about—that you intercede for someone or that you control what you are saying? Sometimes that is the real issue—control.

You will note that the verse in Romans says: "But the Spirit Himself makes intercession for us with groanings which cannot be uttered." As that is translated into English, it does not seem to make sense. After all, how can you have a "groaning" if it cannot be "uttered?" A more accurate translation would be: "But the Spirit Himself makes intercession for us with groanings that cannot be uttered *in articulate speech.*" Again, you won't know what you are praying about, but that is fine. You may be praying for someone on the other side of the world, even someone you don't even know, but the Spirit knows that person needs intercession. There will be no need for you to pat yourself on the back or give yourself credit for praying for that person.

In the past, I've compared this to *transmitting* on a different radio band. When you tune in a radio on AM, you cannot hear music or talk radio that is currently being broadcast on FM radio—but it's there all the same. Likewise, when you set your radio to FM, you cannot hear AM wavelengths. Prayer in the Holy Spirit is the same thing: your prayers are *broadcast* to God in a language you can't decipher, but the good news is that the devil can't figure out what you are praying, either. As a result, he can't interfere, divert you, or infect a prayer with racism, personal animosity, or any other impurity.

At the end of *Bruce Almighty*, Bruce finally realizes he loves Grace so much that he would willingly lose her if she could only be happy. God asks Bruce if he wants her back, and he replies, "No. I want her to be happy, no matter what that means. I want her to find someone who will treat her with all the love she deserved from me. I want her to meet someone who will see her always as I do now, through Your eyes."

God smiles and say, "Now *that's* a prayer." How often, though, can we, with a completely pure heart, pray such things, especially if our will for a person or a situation isn't what God has in mind? If your son or daughter wants to marry a person of a different race or income level, can you pray, "Lord, I want my son or daughter to be happy and to love that person just as You love him or her"? Often we can't even pray that about a person our son or daughter brings home of the *same* race or income level. This is precisely why God gave us the intercessory prayer of the Holy Spirit.

Finally, intercessory prayer (regardless of whether you pray in your native tongue or in the Spirit) can only work if it is in line with God's plans and His law. The Holy Spirit guarantees that for us, running a *scan*, if you will, on God's plan for a person or a situation. It is a can't-lose proposition.

## 6. THE PRAYER OF BINDING AND LOOSING

This prayer is found in Matthew 18:18–19, where Jesus says:

> Assuredly, I say to you, whatever you bind on earth will
> be bound in heaven, and whatever you loose on earth
> will be loosed in heaven. Again I say to you that if two
> of you agree on earth concerning anything that they
> ask, it will be done for them by My Father in heaven.

There are several important nuggets in Jesus's statements here, with the first being that we have authority *here on this earth* by virtue of our covenant rights through Jesus.

The second thing we notice is the *direction* of the action. Things do not begin in heaven and come to earth, but rather the action starts here on earth. Notice that it says, "Whatever you bind on earth will be bound in heaven, and whatever you loose on earth will be loosed in heaven." Like all things in God's system, this prayer only works in line with God's Word and His laws. You cannot *bind* things willy-nilly. Binding a team to lose in the Super Bowl won't work any more than loosing someone to love you will work. You can bind foul spirits that are at work in people's lives or loose angelic spirits to work on your behalf in those areas where God has already promised you results. When you pray in that manner, God affirms it in heaven and puts His seal of approval on your prayer. Binding and loosing have to be based on the authority that God has granted you in Scripture, not on some desire you have.

## LEARNING TO USE YOUR PRAYER TOOLS

Those are the six types of prayer that you find in the Bible. They constitute our prayer "tools." When you want to address a problem through prayer, you must use the right tool, or you will be spinning your ratchet around uselessly forever. There may be times when it is appropriate to mix together some of these prayer tools. It is perfectly all right to pray in agreement (where you are certain of the other party's confession) and also say a prayer of intercession. We see an example of this in Colossians 1:3–12. Paul begins with a prayer of worship and praise: "We give thanks to the God and Father of our Lord Jesus Christ" (v. 3). Then he follows with intercessory prayer: "…praying always for you." He notes that "…we heard of your faith in Christ Jesus" (v. 4), then gives a historical lesson over the next few verses. In verse 9, however, he returns to the news of their faith:

> For this reason we also, since the day we heard it [i.e., that you have believed], do not cease to pray for you, and ask that you may be filled with the knowledge of His will in all wisdom and spiritual understanding; that you may walk worthy of the Lord, fully pleasing Him, being fruitful in every good work and increasing in the knowledge of God; strengthened with all might, according to His glorious power, for all patience and long suffering with joy; giving thanks to the Father who has qualified us to be partakers of the inheritance of the saints in the light.
>
> —COLOSSIANS 1:9–12

Part of this is intercessory prayer. Paul is praying for them to receive these things and to be blessed, but obviously Paul knows what these people want. They either told him, wrote to him, or otherwise expressed (maybe to a traveling evangelist) what their desires were. They wanted to be "filled with the knowledge of His will in all wisdom and spiritual understanding...being fruitful," and so on. How much of this is intercession (Paul praying *for them*) and how much is agreement (Paul praying *with them*) isn't clear, but it's a good example of a mixed prayer that meets all the requirements. Note also that in his prayer for them, Paul teaches them how to pray ("giving thanks to the Father"). He emphasized to them to pray with thanksgiving.

In 1 Timothy, Paul instructed Timothy: "That supplications, prayers, intercessions, and giving of thanks be made for all men, for kings and all who are in authority, that we may lead a quiet and peaceable life in all godliness and reverence" (1 Tim. 2:1–2). So Paul tells us that part of our prayer life, whether through thanks or intercessions, should be "for all men." He means *on behalf of all men,* since all men are not saved and do not have the privilege of coming to God. He also tells us to pray for "kings and all who are in authority." If you are not praying for your president, legislators, governor, judges, police, and fire personnel, you need to be. You should do this whether you voted for them or not, because it is your life that will be in trouble if they do a bad job. Paul says we pray for them "that we may lead a quiet and peaceable life in all godliness and reverence." Here in Los Angeles we have had our share of riots, and they are not very peaceable. It's worth noting that Paul said you can pray for these people either through giving thanks—"Father, thank You that I live in a great country where I am free to worship You without fear of violent retribution." Or you can pray for others through intercession: "Father, guide and bless our (fill in the blank here—president, governor, mayor) with wisdom and understanding that I might live a peaceful life."

> While you may use more than one
> prayer tool at any given time, you
> need to be clear on which tool you
> are using, as well as its limitations.

Paul also addresses not only the structure of prayer but also the "when." In 1 Thessalonians 5:17, Paul repeats a phrase that he used in Colossians as an instruction: "Pray without ceasing." Earlier he had said, "We do not cease to pray for you" (Col. 1:9). In 1 Thessalonians, Paul is teaching by doing, then showing the people what he did.

In 2 Thessalonians 3:1–2, Paul tells the church at Thessalonica *how* to pray for him, telling them what he and they could pray in agreement about: "Finally, brethren, pray for us, that the word of the Lord may run swiftly and be glorified, just as it is with you, and that we may be delivered from unreasonable and wicked men; for not all have faith." In verse 4, he adds, "And we have confidence in the Lord concerning you, both that you do and will do the things we command you." What did he just "command" them to do? To pray for Paul and his companions, and he had faith the Thessalonians would do so.

Each of these prayer tools God has provided has a specific purpose. While you may use more than one at any given time, you need to be clear on which tool you are using, as well as its limitations. Given that we have His Word—the Bible—there is no reason for us not to use them properly.

# Reflections From "Use the Right Tool"

# CHAPTER TWO

# HOW DID JESUS PRAY?

*And in that day you will ask Me nothing. Most
assuredly, I say to you, whatever you ask the
Father in My name He will give you. Until now
you have asked nothing in my name. Ask, and
you will receive, that your joy may be full!*
—John 16:23–24

We have looked at several types of prayer listed in the Bible and found that there are important differences in what the Father had in mind when He designed these prayers. Each type of prayer fits a particular set of rules, and one prayer would not be appropriate in another circumstance. The best model of prayer, however, would be the example of the Lord Jesus Himself. How did He pray when He was on the earth? And what would be His model for an "answered prayer"?

We can look at John 14 for some answers. In John 14:12–14, Jesus, speaking to the disciples, said:

Most assuredly, I say to you, he who believes in Me, the works that I do he will do also; and greater works than

39

these he will do, because I go to My Father. And whatever you ask in My name, that I will do, that the Father may be glorified in the Son. If you ask anything in My name, I will do it.

## YOUR AUTHORITY AS A BELIEVER

Before we look at the specific meaning of these verses, I want to point out that while all the words in the Bible are divinely inspired, the pages, page numbering, chapter divisions, and even the punctuation are the work of the translators. There is nothing "divine" about the chapter and verse divisions—those are welcome conveniences that help us find things. Originally, however, the books of the Bible were letters, written on scrolls, without English punctuation.

I say this because in verse 12, there is a period after "My Father," followed by another phrase in verse 13—"And whatever you ask in My name, that I will do, that the Father may be glorified in the Son." The period in this case tends to stop the flow. Another way this could be read might say: "Most assuredly I say to you, He who believes in Me, the works that I do he will do also; and greater works than these will he do, because I go to My Father, and whatever you ask in my name, that I will do, that the Father may be glorified in the Son." I submit to you that this portion of Scripture does not refer to prayer but to doing works in the name of Jesus.

The greatest work possible is leading
someone from spiritual death into
spiritual life in Jesus Christ. That
is our awesome privilege. Jesus
could never do that, but we can!

Are there other verses that support this? In John 14:10, Jesus said, "Do you not believe that I am in the Father, and the Father in Me? The words that I speak to you I do not speak on my own authority; but the Father who dwells in Me does the works." Notice the word *works*. We see it again in verses 12–13: "Most assuredly, I say to you, he who believes in Me, the works that I do he will do also; and greater works than these he will do, because I go to My Father. And whatever you ask in My name, that I will do, that the Father may be glorified in the Son."

Note here Jesus did not say "that your needs may be met" or that "you shall have what you asked for."

The root word *aiteo,* in verse 13, is not "ask," but more appropriately "demand." (*Strong's Dictionary of the Bible* defines *aiteo* as "strictly a demand for something due," in NT:4441; see NT:154.) Verse 13 really says, "And whatever you demand in My name, that I will do." You cannot demand anything of God—which tells me this verse refers to the believer's authority over Satan. What you would be doing, in accordance with John 14:13, is demanding that Satan obey,

41

through the authority of the name of Jesus. In fact, John tells us that Jesus meant for us to do even more, or "greater," works than He did. Jesus raised the dead, opened blind eyes, cast out demons, cleansed lepers, calmed the storm, and fed multitudes with a few fishes and loaves. How can we do "greater" works than He did?

By "greater," Jesus meant "the same, but more, multiplied many times over." He could only heal a few lepers at a time and deal with those in His immediate presence, because He was limited by a physical body. He was one person, but we are many millions. If all of us operate in the gifts of the Spirit, then we should be healing people by the multitudes—in essence, doing all that He did, but because there are more of us, doing it more frequently and in more locations at a time.

I ask the question again: "How can we do greater than Jesus?" Consider this: During the earthly ministry of the Lord Jesus, He never was instrumental in getting anyone saved. In other words, He never led anyone into receiving Jesus Christ as personal Savior and Lord. (See Romans 10:9–10.) Why? He couldn't because He hadn't died yet and been raised from the dead. The greatest work possible is leading someone from spiritual death into spiritual life in Jesus Christ. That is our awesome privilege. Jesus could never do that, but we can!

There *is* something about Jesus's
name, and for believers, it is
a divine legal instrument that
we need to use responsibly.

*Demanding* something in Jesus's name means that when we encounter satanic oppression, such as a person captive to the devil in some area, we have authority over the devil (through Jesus) and can demand that the devil release that person in the name of Jesus. Let me give you an illustration of how this works. Say that God calls me, as pastor of Crenshaw Christian Center, to a ministry mission to China. I must be away from the church for many months, but the operation of the church must still go on. Sermons must be preached, bills must be paid, and so on. While I'm gone, I can delegate my son, Frederick, under the law to conduct business in my absence through what's called the "power of attorney." He can sign checks in my name and conclude contracts in my name; from a legal point of view, it is as though I were there doing those things.

When Jesus left to go to heaven, He gave us the power of attorney to conduct kingdom business in His name. We don't do this on our own authority. Do you remember when, in Acts 19:13–16, the seven sons of Sceva, who tried to go around exorcising demons, came to one demon-possessed fellow who said, "Jesus I know, and Paul I know, but who are you?" He leaped on them and gave them what we here in America call a "whuppin'." Those men had no *authority* to use the name of Jesus, and the demons knew it. Another way of putting that is, "I know the name of Jesus, and I know Paul, because he has authority to use that name, and he has used it on us before, but you don't have any right to use that name."

Using the name of Jesus is not only a great privilege, but it is also a magnificent responsibility. If you want to accomplish anything—if you want to get results—you must use the name of Jesus when it comes to spiritual matters. When you do, Satan and all the demons say, "Jesus I know!" and back off. The Lord may not physically be here, but His authority is here.

I want to make it very clear that these verses, in my opinion, are not referring to prayer, but they involve our use of heavenly authority to conduct business here on earth. Too often we fail to use the name of Jesus effectively or with faith. You have heard the song "There's Just Something About That Name." It's true, there *is* something about His name, and for believers, it is a divine legal instrument that we need to use responsibly. We see that in Acts 3:1–8, where John and Peter encounter a lame beggar. Peter said, "Silver and gold I do not have, but what I do have I give you: In the name of Jesus Christ of Nazareth, rise up and walk" (v. 6). We do not know that Peter meant that he was dead broke—I'm not certain of that at all—but rather when he said, "Silver and gold I do not have," he meant, "I don't have money that will address your real problem, which is that you can't walk." The critical part comes when he says, "In the *name* of Jesus Christ of Nazareth, rise up and walk." At that moment, the demons of infirmity and lameness that had

44

afflicted that man all those years said, in essence, "The name of Jesus, I know!"—and out they went. Peter went on to address the people who gathered around by saying:

> The God of Abraham, Isaac, and Jacob, the God of our fathers, glorified His Servant Jesus, whom you delivered up and denied in the presence of Pilate, when he was determined to let Him go.
>
> —ACTS 3:13

What did we read in John 14? "Whatever you ask [demand] in My name, that will I do, that the Father may be glorified in the Son."

Do you see the difference? Peter wasn't praying for the lame man; he was laying hands on him and exercising authority in the name of Jesus. Peter did not get down on his knees and say, "O Lord, Thou who has been our dwelling place in all the generations, before the mountains were brought forth, or ever Thou haddest formed the earth and the world, even from everlasting to everlasting, Thou art God! O Lord, hear our humble prayer. Have mercy on this lame man, Lord, if it be Thy will." No! Peter invoked the name of Jesus Christ of Nazareth, saying, "Stand up and walk." In essence, Peter was announcing to the devil, "Take your filthy hands off this son of Israel. You bind him no more!"

> Don't pray "in the name of Charlene."
> That isn't going to work! To the
> demons of hell, there is only *one*
> *name* that carries any weight—the
> name of Jesus Christ of Nazareth.

Note that Peter did not even try to use his own authority. He did not merely say, "Rise up and walk." Peter's name, by itself, carried no authority. The demons might say, "Jesus I know, and Paul I know, and Peter I know," but with Paul and Peter and the rest of us, they *only* "know" us by the authority of the name of Jesus, not by any power we have in ourselves. In Acts 10:38, Luke tells us, "God anointed Jesus of Nazareth with the Holy Spirit and with power, who went about doing good and healing all who were oppressed by the devil, for God was with Him." Sickness and disease are forms of satanic oppression, and we have authority over them. But don't try "in the name of Charlene" or "in the name of Eric" or "in the name of "Carlos." That isn't going to work! Your parents might like your names, and they might be beautiful names full of symbolic meaning, but to the demons of hell, there is only *one name* that carries any weight—the name of Jesus Christ of Nazareth.

## HOW TO USE YOUR AUTHORITY IN JESUS

If the only way we can pray is in the name of Jesus, then we need to know, "How did Jesus pray?" I know many of you will almost immediately think of the Lord's Prayer. I will save the discussion of the Lord's Prayer for later, but I do not consider that to be the *model prayer* for a Christian.

What instructions did Jesus give *us*—the believers—for the time after He had ascended? You will find that in John 16:23, where Jesus, speaking to His disciples, says, "And in *that day*..." Right there we have to stop and ask, what "day" does He mean? It is obvious that if He said, "in *that* day" then He did not mean "in *this* day" (the day in which He was living). Put another way, He was contrasting the future (from the time He was speaking) to the present in which He spoke. Another way of putting this would be to say, "In the future..."

This is a little-discussed point, but note that in the three and a half years we have any record of, the disciples never one time prayed to the Father for anything. Whenever they needed something, they asked Jesus for it. I mean, why would you drive a hundred miles to the company warehouse to buy some shaving cream when the local store owned by that company has it a half mile down the block? Jesus was right there with them. Anything they needed, He supplied it. When the waves crashed in on their boat, they awoke Him and said, "Save us, Lord!" When someone was sick, they said, "Lord, this person is ill. Please heal him." Whatever it was, they asked it of Him directly, not of God the Father.

47

So it is significant that when we read John 16:23, we find Jesus, after explaining to them that He was going to the Father soon, saying, "And in that day you will ask Me nothing. Most assuredly, I say to you, whatever you ask the Father in My name He will give you." Remember, just a little earlier in John 14:14 we read: "If you ask anything in My name, I will do it [for you]." Yet here He says, "Don't ask Me anything, but instead ask the Father in My name."

He elaborates on this in verse 24: "Until now you have asked nothing in My name. Ask [or a better translation is, "Ask now," or "Ask, after this point, in My name"], and you will receive, that your joy may be full." Do you see the difference? While Jesus was with them physically, they asked *Him*. But soon after Jesus said those words, He would not be with them anymore, and they would have to ask *the Father in His name*. Why couldn't they ask the Father in His name while Jesus still walked with them? Jesus had not delegated that name to them yet. He hadn't died and risen from the dead.

Notice also that Jesus said, "You will receive, that [or, "in order that"] your joy may be full." God wants us to have full joy. Not just *tolerable* joy or partial joy, but *full* joy. Full joy is when your pantry is well stocked and you aren't hungry every night. Full joy is when your car works and can take you to your job without breaking down. Full joy is when your body is whole and you aren't battling sickness and disease every day. That does not mean that you should not be joyful when circumstances are not perfect, but that is not God's best for you.

In these verses we have the "how to pray" from Jesus: "And in that day you will ask Me nothing. Most assuredly, I say to you, whatever you *ask the Father in My name...*" tells us everything we need to know about how to pray. That is the key that starts the *car* of faith, if you will.

You need to know what to do with that car once it's running, and you need to know what to pray *for* after you begin your prayer, *but this is the formula for an answered prayer.* You are to "ask the Father in My name." Do not ask Jesus. Unless you are engaging in praise and worship ("Thank You, Jesus, for Your sacrifice," or "Praise You, Jesus, that You are King of kings and Lord of lords"), you do not pray to Jesus. He said so. Instead, you are to direct your requests to the Father in Jesus's name. It's like a letter. "Heavenly Father" is the introduction, the "Dear So-and-So," and "In the name of Jesus" is your signature line. You sign your prayer in His name, not your own. Your name doesn't carry any weight in the spirit world. Just try healing the sick in the name of Tom, or in the name of Cheryl, or in the name of Buddha, and see who gets healed! Those names do not have the authority to heal anyone. What you put in between the "introduction" and the "signature" is all you.

---

Whatever situation it is, you cannot base a prayer on what you want to have happen, but only on what is promised to you by God in His Word.

---

This is why I dealt with the verse from Romans 8:26 in the first chapter. ("Likewise the Spirit also helps our weaknesses. For we do not know what we should pray for as we ought, but the Spirit Himself makes intercession for us with groanings which cannot be uttered.") Paul tells us that sometimes we do not know *"what we should pray for"* as we should. He did not say that we did not know "how to pray."

What do you pray for? I'll deal with that in a separate chapter, as it is one of the basics of answered prayer, but the simple answer is twofold:

1. What do you need?
2. Does God's Word promise you that?

If you think you "need" an adulterous affair, then forget it. God's Word does not promise you that, and you will have no success whatsoever praying to receive that. But if you need a stronger marriage, the Bible is full of promises that a believer's marriage should be blessed. Maybe there is a bully who has been harming your child. You cannot pray that God kill that bully—the Bible doesn't give you that authority. But it does promise that your enemies will come at you one way and go away fleeing seven ways (Deut. 28:7). If your child isn't old enough or spiritually mature enough to claim that for himself or herself, you can pray that over him or her. You cannot pray that a business rival will go broke. The Word doesn't promise you that. But it does promise in Deuteronomy that you will be blessed in the city and blessed in the country, that the Lord will increase your cattle and your flocks (since we don't deal in cattle today, substitute the words "bank accounts and bond portfolios"), and that the Lord will command the blessing on you in your storehouses (i.e., in your savings accounts). What happens to your rival should be of no concern if your business is prospering beyond all your hopes and dreams! The greatest businessmen in American history uniformly focused on themselves and their production, never on their rivals. Whatever situation it is, you cannot base a prayer on what you want to have happen, but only on what is promised to you by God in His Word.

So what is the "how to" part of prayer? *Address your requests to the Father, in the name of Jesus.*

There is a big push right now to secularize Christian prayers in public settings and to remove the name of Jesus from the end of the prayer. I can tell you right now that those prayers will be utterly devoid of power without that *signature*. Without the name of Jesus, no person—regardless of their religious background or persuasion—can pray a petition prayer and expect God to act on it. However, God will always respond to a prayer of redemption and acceptance of His Son. ("Lord, I accept Your Son as my Lord and Savior.") So from that perspective, He will always hear the prayer of anyone—Christian, Jew, Muslim, Buddhist, or atheist—as long as that person's prayer is one of acceptance of Jesus. But the name of Jesus is the only name that has any authority or gets any action from a prayer.

## What About the "Lord's Prayer"?

If John 16:23–24 is the *model prayer* from Jesus's perspective, and if that's what He gave us as a blueprint, then we need to discuss what is traditionally called the "Lord's Prayer." Many people think that *it* is the blueprint for praying. This issue is quite sensitive for some people, and my purpose is not to tread on people's beliefs or kick sacred cows. However, it is important that we correct error where we find it.

Matthew 6:9–13 is traditionally called the "Lord's Prayer." This passage begins with Jesus speaking to His disciples:

> In this manner, therefore, pray:
>
> Our Father in heaven,
> Hallowed be Your name.
> Your kingdom come.
> Your will be done
> On earth as it is in heaven.
> Give us this day our daily bread.
> And forgive us our debts,
> As we forgive our debtors.
> And do not lead us into temptation,
> But deliver us from the evil one.
> For Yours is the kingdom and the power and the glory
> forever. Amen.

I believe that based on what Jesus told us in John, this prayer could not possibly work for us today, and that God the Father could not possibly honor this prayer. If it were a document you were trying to save in a computer, you would get an error message every time you tried to send this. Why? What is the most obvious thing missing from this prayer? "In the name of Jesus."

Notice that Jesus just ended the prayer with *Amen*. Why do you think Jesus did not tell the disciples to pray in His name at that time? He could not yet tell them to pray in His name because that authority had not been delegated yet. He hadn't died and been resurrected yet. Apparently this was written early in His ministry, as it comes at the beginning of Matthew, which most scholars consider to be a historical book.

When you send a prayer request to heaven, it's much like cashing a check at the bank. The angels who work in the teller cages examine the check for a signature that matches the one they have on record. If that signature isn't there, they kick it out. From that perspective alone, the Lord's Prayer would be in conflict with the model prayer that Jesus told us to pray. We have already seen in Acts 19:11–16 what happened when the Jewish exorcists attempted to use the name of Jesus illegitimately. Not only do you have to *sign* the check with the name of Jesus, but you also have to be on the account!

If you pray based on John 16:23–24, the Lord's Prayer won't work. Why not? Because it is not prayed in the name of Jesus. It ends with a simple *Amen*. It is interesting that in the four Gospels, we never once read of the disciples praying this prayer, nor do we read of any believers praying this prayer from Acts to Revelation. We have no record that the disciples ever prayed this or that Paul ever prayed it. Why then would it be a prayer we should pray? Yet we were instructed by Jesus Himself to pray to the Father in Jesus's name.

---

**After Jesus's death and resurrection, we were delivered from the power of darkness, so you are already out of the grip of the evil one.**

---

You may ask, "Well, Dr. Price, why can't we just say, 'In Jesus's name' at the end of the Lord's Prayer?" That is a good question, but there is a simple answer: *Because Jesus didn't say it.* If it was a model prayer for us, then Jesus would have had to do it, and He did not. It would be absolutely inappropriate for you to pray the Lord's Prayer and tack "in Jesus's name" on the end of it.

Furthermore, if the Lord's Prayer was a model prayer, since there are six different kinds of prayer, it would have to be a model for all six kinds of prayer, and it is not. There is nothing about a prayer of agreement, a prayer of consecration and dedication, or about binding and loosing.

So why did Jesus give this prayer to the disciples? Peter, James, and John were not Christians when they walked with Jesus. They were still un-born-again Jews—faithful Jews in the mold of Abraham, but still not born-again men. Moreover, they were students in training. But they could not *graduate* until Jesus died and was resurrected. Until His resurrection, as

I mentioned before, they had no right to use the name. They had not yet been given the "power of attorney."

## CONVEYED INTO THE KINGDOM OF GOD

Let's look again at what Jesus said in regard to prayer. He said:

> Our Father in heaven,
> Hallowed be Your name.
> Your kingdom come.
> Your will be done
> On earth as it is in heaven.
>
> —MATTHEW 6:9–10

Go to that phrase, "Your kingdom come." Can we agree that you can only pray for something to "come" that is not already here? The prayer doesn't say, "Your kingdom has come," but rather "[When] Your kingdom comes, Your will be done," or "[Let] Your kingdom come, [that] Your will be done." In Colossians 1:12–13 we read:

> …giving thanks to the Father who has qualified us to
> be partakers of the inheritance of the saints in the light.
> He has delivered us from the power of darkness and
> conveyed us into the kingdom of the Son of His love.

Another translation says He "has translated us into the kingdom of the Son of his love" (ASV). Paul's letter to the Colossians obviously comes after the Resurrection. It is a part of the New Covenant. But Jesus's comments in Matthew were before the complete establishment of the New Covenant. Really, the

*New Testament* should begin with Romans, not Matthew, because the New Covenant doesn't really start until Jesus is resurrected. But that's another discussion.

---

> Friend, if you had not already been
> delivered from the power of darkness,
> do you think you could rebuke the
> devil and have him flee from you? . . . If
> you are not submitted to God or His
> Word, the devil will not flee from you.

---

The "us" in Colossians 1:12–13 refers to born-again people. He has delivered us from the power of darkness. Would you agree that "delivered" is past tense? That means at one point you needed to be delivered from something, correct? When the Lord's Prayer says "deliver us from evil," does that not suggest that at that time "us" (pardon my grammar, but I want you to see this) were not yet "delivered"? If you still have to pray, "Deliver me from evil" (or more accurately, the "evil one"), then it is safe to say you are not delivered. You must still be under the authority of the evil one.

In Colossians we continue by reading these words: "He has delivered us from the power of darkness and conveyed us into the kingdom of the Son of His love." So not only have we been delivered, but also we have been conveyed (or "translated").

After Jesus's death and resurrection, we were delivered from the power of darkness, so you are already out of the grip of the evil one. James 4:7 tells us: "Therefore submit to God. Resist the devil and he will flee from you." Note it didn't say the devil would flee from God, but from you! Why? Because you have been given the name of Jesus and His authority. It didn't even say pray about the devil, but to resist him—after first submitting yourself to God.

Friend, if you had not already been delivered from the power of darkness, do you think you could rebuke the devil and have him flee from you? Submitting yourself to God means submitting to His Word, because God and His Word are one. But if you are not submitted to God or His Word, the devil will not flee from you. In Mark 16:17, Jesus said, "And these signs will follow those who believe: In My name they will cast out demons; they will speak with new tongues." When Jesus said that believers would "cast out demons," He meant that they would have the authority over malevolent spirits. After the Resurrection, God would not do anything about the devil because He gave *us* the authority to handle the devil in this world. We are told to "rebuke" Satan and to "cast out demons."

An important clue that this power was not already given on a blanket basis when Jesus walked on the earth with His disciples also appears in Mark's verse, where Jesus said: "And these signs will follow..." He did not say, "...have followed and will continue to follow." This authority was only going to come after His resurrection. You may remember that *at times* Jesus delegated that authority when He sent out groups of disciples to proclaim the Good News. (See Luke 9:1.) At the time He delegated that authority, He gave them power (authority) over demons and the power to heal the sick. When the seventy were sent out, even though Luke does not expressly say they were given that same authority over demons, look what they said in Luke 10:17 when they returned: "Lord, even the demons are subject to us in Your name." While He walked with them, He could delegate authority at any time, and it was also clear that the authority was specific to the task at hand.

---

We have been delivered from the evil one and have authority over him. But remember that authority not exercised is as good as no authority at all.

---

When Jesus gave His disciples authority to trample [or tread] on serpents and scorpions, He was not referring to natural reptiles and insects but to spiritual demonic forces (Luke 10:19). The word *authority* in the King James Bible is "power," but the Greek word is *exousia*, meaning "authority." This authority was specifically delegated by Jesus to certain individuals, not spread like a blanket over everyone who used His name as he or she pleased. And it had to be mixed with faith. Authority was over the *ability* of the enemy, but it had to be exercised, and it had to be used as directed. In Matthew 17:16–21, we see that a man came to Jesus with his epileptic son, but he had first taken the boy to the disciples, who "could not cure him." Why not? Jesus later said to them it was because of their unbelief, making a point about faith.

Until that moment when Jesus arose from the dead, no one had yet been delivered from the evil one. But since the resurrection of Jesus, we do not need to ever question whether we have been granted that authority. If you have accepted the salvation offered through Jesus's death and resurrection, *you have been delivered from the evil one.* You may need to *receive* that revelation. Perhaps you have been taught that you are just an *old sinner*, a *helpless worm*, and powerless. If so, you may need deliverance from wrong doctrine. You may need to be aware that you have authority through Jesus, and you must, by all means, act on it for it to work, but you don't need to pray to be delivered from Satan; *you are delivered.* My friends, if a package is delivered at your door from Aunt Beatrice just in time for Christmas, you do not get on the phone and call Aunt Beatrice and say, "When are you going to deliver my package?" She already has! We have been delivered from the evil one and have authority over him. But remember that authority not exercised is as good as no authority at all.

When Jesus said, "It is finished," from the cross of Calvary, the veil in the temple was torn in half, ending the Old Covenant. Until that moment, man had not been able to go to God directly, but he needed a priest to act as an intermediary. At that moment on the cross, the Old Covenant was finished. Jesus was not talking about salvation when He uttered those three words. For some years I preached that when Jesus said, "It is finished," it meant that man's salvation was accomplished. NO! Only the Law as binding on man was finished at the cross of Calvary. Salvation was not accomplished until three days later when Jesus arose from the grave.

Moreover, we learned that Jesus also "conveyed us into the kingdom of the Son of His love." We have already been conveyed into the kingdom. Just as in the case of "delivering" us, if we have been conveyed into the kingdom, how can we pray, "Your kingdom come"? Imagine if this verse had said Jesus took us by airplane to Los Angeles. Would you pray, "Los Angeles come," or "May You bring me to Los Angeles," if you are *already there?* The *kingdom* is not our heavenly life after death; God's kingdom is here, now, within us.

It is very clear to me from an understanding of these points that the Lord's Prayer was a different prayer, for a different time, for a different group of people than the types of prayer I outlined in chapter one. Jesus was answering a request from one of His disciples to teach them to pray *at the time when Jesus still walked with them.* Since they did not (yet) have the authority of His name, and since He had not empowered them with the Holy Spirit because He had not yet died and been resurrected, this was a model prayer for them—at that particular time. But it is not a prayer for us today. Jesus gave the disciples this prayer to finish out the Old Covenant.

## DEATH WAS NOT PART OF GOD'S ORIGINAL PLAN

Now look at Hebrews 2:14–15:

60

Inasmuch then as the children have partaken of flesh and blood, He Himself likewise shared in the same, that through death He might destroy him who had the power of death, that is, the devil, and release those who through fear of death were all their lifetime subject to bondage.

Note that "as the children," we have already "partaken" of flesh and blood. That's past tense. And Jesus "Himself likewise shared in the same." "Shared" is past tense. So these things already happened. Why did they happen? "That through death He might destroy him who had the power of death, that is, the devil." Or a more colloquial way of putting it would be, "So that through death" or "In order that through death He might destroy him who had the power of death, that is, the devil."

---

Jesus released us from both the death and the fear. That does not mean that most Christians are automatically free from the fear of death, even though they are free from the death, because fear is a choice.

---

The reason Jesus "likewise shared in the same" (the "same" meaning "flesh and blood" referred to in verse 14) was in order for Jesus to destroy the devil, because the devil had the power of death. Note the use of the word *had*. Not "has," but past tense. Satan *had* the power of death until Jesus "likewise" became a man and died and rose again, destroying the power of death.

If you remember, death was not in God's original plan in the Garden. If Adam had not yielded to the temptation presented to him through Eve, he never would have died. But once he ate of the fruit, death had authority over man— and he who had authority over death, the devil, likewise had authority over man. God—again, purely from a legal stand-point—was powerless to intervene. Let me give you an example in real life as to how this works. If you have a daughter, she is your child, at least until she becomes an adult, and she is your responsibility. However, if she marries some man and legally becomes his wife, you lose almost all *legal* authority over her. For example, he may convince her to join the Scien-tologists, and there isn't a thing you can legally do about it. Or maybe she had a trust fund—some money you laid aside for her—and she can sign it over to him, and you have no legal control over the disposition of that money. When Adam disregarded God, he gave legal authority over his life to the devil. And we inherited that legal relationship, so the minute you are born, you begin using up life. Even as a little baby, you are getting closer to death with every breath you take.

If we are constantly speaking faith,
and our friends are speaking unbelief,
then we may have a problem. We
might have to choose between our
spiritual well-being and our friends.

Paul writes that Jesus partook in our flesh and blood that He might destroy death "and release those who through fear of death were all their lifetime subject to bondage." We were bound to death and the fear of death, but Jesus released us from both the death and the fear. That does not mean that most Christians are automatically free from the fear of death, even though they are free from the death, because fear is a choice. There are people who are afraid of flying on airplanes, and if you ask them why, and if they are honest, they will tell you it is because they are afraid of dying in an airplane crash. They have been delivered from death, but they are still in bondage to the fear. You might have an insurance settlement check waiting for you at the bank to come in and affix your signature to, and that check might make you free from debt. But you will still be afraid of debt if you never go and actually sign that check. Those bills will still come, even though on paper you have money waiting for you.

Let's deal with another word found in Hebrews 2, which is the word *destroy*. Normal usage of that word implies "obliterated or annihilated—totally wiped out, so that it does not exist any longer." If that was a correct translation of "destroy," it would mean that by His resurrection, Jesus had *killed* ("destroy") the devil. That is not the case. The Book of Revelation makes it clear that the devil is around until the final curtain falls.

In the original Greek, the word *destroy* means "to abolish, to deliver from, to do away with, to loose, or to bring to nothing, to make void." In other words, Jesus has eliminated and abolished and brought to nothing the authority of the devil, but He has not yet killed off or exterminated Satan. So that old dude is still around to tempt you and attack you, but if you know your legal rights in Christ, you do not have to accept his attacks. You have authority over him. You must know you have that authority, however, and use it. Hosea 4:6 says, "My people are destroyed for lack of knowledge." Destruction comes, not for lack of authority or power, but for a lack of how to use that authority or power.

In Ephesians 4:27 we have yet another verse telling us we already have been delivered from the power of the evil one, where it says: "...nor give place to the devil." That means we have the authority to deny the devil a place in our lives. If we had not been delivered from the evil one, we would have no ability or authority to deny him a place. On a practical, daily basis, this requires us to search our lives to see if we are giving the devil any piece of territory, any turf, that he can use as a base to attack our lives.

Do you have an addiction or habit? Can that be used as a beachhead by Satan? Are you eating the wrong things? This is one reason I say grace before every meal, no matter where I am—I'm not going to allow the enemy to come at me through food. You don't know who cooked that meal or where it's been! You don't know what was fed to the animals or what was sprayed on the vegetables. It's not possible for you to check all that out, either, so you better bless your food and give it some prayer protection.

The word *place*, as it's used in Ephesians 4:27, comes from the Greek word *topos*, from which we get our modern word *topography*. This refers to the lay of the land—mountains, lakes, rocks, and so on. Paul's intent here is that we should not give the evil one a single rock, not a nook or a cranny, to use as a base from which to attack us. This includes our associates— those whom we hang out with. Some of our friends may not be so good for us. If we are constantly speaking faith, and they are speaking unbelief, if we are talking healing, and they are talking disease, then we may have a problem. We might have to choose between our spiritual well-being and our friends.

We have discussed several reasons why Christians should use John 16:23–24 as a model of how Jesus prayed, and not the Lord's Prayer.

1. As believers, we have already been delivered from the evil one, so it indicates a lack of faith (or a lack of understanding) to keep praying, "Deliver us from evil" or "Deliver us from the evil one."

2. We have already been "translated" into the kingdom of God's dear Son, so it is misguided to continue to pray, "Thy kingdom come."

3. Jesus said to ask the Father for those things that we need in His name, yet the Lord's Prayer does not end in the *signature*—"In Jesus's name." It would be spiritually incorrect to tack that phrase on.

## A TEMPORARY MODEL OF PRAYER

There is one more good indicator that this prayer is not for post-Resurrection Christians.

Think about this—we call this the "Lord's Prayer." If it's the Lord's Prayer, what are you doing with it? If you see a car that belongs to Greg, it isn't your car. It seems logical that you would want your own prayer. But if it is the *Lord's Prayer*, then it isn't *your* prayer.

I submit to you that the Lord's Prayer was a temporary model for the disciples for that brief time when Jesus walked with them on the earth. They could ask Him (without petition prayer) for anything they needed, yet the kingdom had not fully arrived yet, and they did not yet have permanent, unalterable authority over the devil, because Jesus had not yet defeated him by rising from the grave. The Old Covenant was over—Jesus was there among them (God among men). But they still needed to pray, and they still had that deep desire to communicate with the Father. So, in the Lord's Prayer, Jesus gave them an intermediary step. But He left them with the model prayer in John 16:23–24 to use after He was raised from the dead. Later in this book we will also look at the example of Mark 11:23–24.

If, after this analysis, you still are not persuaded, then feel free to pray the Lord's Prayer. But based on the instructions Jesus gave us, I cannot see how you would receive any answer to any requests you have if you invoke that prayer model.

## How Did Jesus Pray?

So how did Jesus pray? Look at John 11, where we have the story of Jesus raising Lazarus from the dead. Lazarus of Bethany and his sisters, Mary and Martha, were good friends of Jesus. When Lazarus got sick, the sisters sent a message to Jesus, saying, "Lord, behold, he whom You love is sick" (John 11:3).

Jesus replied: "This sickness is not unto death, but for the glory of God, that the Son of God may be glorified through it" (v. 4). Nevertheless, Jesus did not go to Lazarus immediately, but He waited two more days "in the place where He was" (v. 6). By the time He went to Bethany, Lazarus had been dead four days, and his body had already begun to decompose.

---

Closing your eyes, bowing your head, kneeling, or falling on your face may all help to *focus* you, but in and of themselves they are meaningless.

---

Note that when Jesus heard the news of Lazarus's sickness, the first thing He said was words of faith: "This sickness is not unto death" (v. 4). Wasn't this the Son of God?

Wasn't Jesus a prophet? Couldn't He figure out that Lazarus was dying and certainly would be dead when He got there? Of course, but Jesus also spoke His faith when He said that the sickness is "not unto death," or, put another way, "this sickness won't permanently result in death." Look at the second thing that Jesus said in regard to Lazarus: "Our friend Lazarus sleeps, but I go that I may wake him up." Jesus further confessed His faith by "calling those things which be not as though they were."

In Romans, Paul refers to Abraham's faith by saying that God, "whom he [Abraham] believed...gives life to the dead and calls those things which do not exist as though they did" (Rom. 4:17). Jesus speaks just as God does: He called Lazarus asleep (which did not exist—yet) instead of dead. He called those things that did not (yet) exist as though they did.

Now, sometimes the disciples seemed a little thick. They said, "Lord, if he's asleep we'll just wake him up" (John 11:13). But Jesus spoke of his death. Jesus was trying to teach them a faith lesson, but they weren't ready to receive it yet. So Jesus had to tell them plainly, "Lazarus is dead" (v. 14). Then He continued by saying: "And I am glad for your sakes that I was not there, that you may believe. Nevertheless let us go to him" (v. 15). Here Jesus was trying to tell them, "If I had been there, I would have healed him, but you are about to see a much greater miracle than a mere healing."

When Jesus arrived on the scene, He asked where they had placed Him. Then He said, "Take away the stone" (v. 39).

Martha wanted to argue with Him, saying, "Lord, by this time there is a stench, for he has been dead four days" (v. 39). But Jesus said, "Did I not say to you that if you would believe you would see the glory of God?" (v. 40).

So they rolled away the stone, and we read this remarkable statement:

> And Jesus lifted up His eyes, and said, "Father, I thank You that You have heard Me. And I know that You always hear Me, but because of the people who are standing by I said this, that they may believe that You sent Me." Now when He had said these things, He cried with a loud voice, "Lazarus, come forth!"
>
> —JOHN 11:41–43

And when He said those words, Lazarus came out of the tomb. Notice that Jesus did not bow His head to pray, but "lifted up His eyes." Notice that He wasn't kneeling. There is nothing at all wrong with kneeling or with bowing your head, but your posture is not as important as the form and process you use. He didn't even close His eyes! Closing your eyes, bowing your head, kneeling, or falling on your face may all help to *focus* you, but in and of themselves they are meaningless.

Here is the key passage to this whole story of Lazarus: "Father, I thank You that You have heard Me." Did you catch that? It's a small thing, and easy to miss, but Jesus said "heard," not "I thank You that You *hear* Me." When do you think God "heard" Jesus? God heard Jesus four days before, in verse 4, where Jesus said, "This sickness is not unto death." He made a confession of faith four days before, then along the way, in verse 11, He said, "Our friend Lazarus sleeps." He didn't say, "Our friend Lazarus has died." That was Jesus's second confession of faith in believing what He had prayed for, namely Lazarus's life. He called those things that were not as though they were.

When it was clear that the disciples were confused, He said, more or less, "Look, dudes, the guy is dead. D-E-A-D, OK? But for your sakes I'm going to do something that will strengthen your faith even more than if I had been there and healed him when he first got sick." Jesus knew that some people would say, "Well, Lazarus really wasn't very sick. Jesus just healed him of a cold."

So He said to His disciples, "I want you disciples to see that this guy is at room temperature and is decaying. Then you'll really see a miracle!"

## Seeing Death as God Sees It

It is important to see death as God sees it. God never sees His people who physically die as dead, but rather asleep. Sleep presupposes that the person will wake up. That will, in fact, happen when the trumpet sounds and Jesus returns. At that point, the dead in Christ will rise. At any rate, when speaking of Lazarus, Jesus *said*, "This sickness is not unto death." He could have merely thought it, and if something went wrong, no one would know. He had to speak His faith for it to work.

You may think that it was because of Jesus's position as the Son of God that He was able to say, "I thank You, Father, that You always hear Me when I pray." But Jesus did not say that because He was arrogant, nor did He say it because He was the Son of God. He said it because that is the way God's Word works—and it never fails. God answers our prayers because we pray according to His Word. Jesus knew that, Paul knew that, and now you know that too.

John 11:41–42 is an example of Jesus praying a petition prayer, or the prayer of faith. We also have an example of Jesus praying a prayer of consecration and dedication in the Garden of Gethsemane, where He said: "O My Father, if it is possible, let this cup pass from Me; nevertheless, not as I will, but as You will" (Matt. 26:39). This example is a clear case of Jesus saying He did not know if it was possible for the cup to pass away from Him. Was it possible that, like Abraham, God would "stay the knife" at the last minute? So Jesus said, "If it is possible... nevertheless..." He was ready to be the sacrifice if it was not possible for God to change the plan. In verse 42, He concluded His prayer by saying, "Your will be done."

Thus we have seen Jesus in two different prayer situations: one, a petition prayer where Lazarus was raised from the dead, and the other, in a prayer of consecration and dedication. But we have no biblical example of Jesus ever praying the Lord's Prayer in similar situations.

## JESUS'S LONGEST RECORDED PRAYER

The longest prayer by Jesus recorded in the Bible takes up all of the seventeenth chapter of John. Let me cover some of the main points in that chapter.

1. Jesus reaffirms that God has "given" Jesus "authority over all flesh, that He should give eternal life to as many as You have given Him" (vv. 1–2).

2. Jesus prayed that God would glorify Him "together with Yourself, with the glory which I had with You before the world was" (v. 5).

3. He then switched gears and began to pray for the disciples, stating that they belonged to Him and to the Father, and that although He was leaving, "these are in the world." He reminded the Father that while they were with Him, He lost none except Judas (the "son of perdition"), "that the Scripture might be fulfilled" (vv. 11–12).

4. In verse 13, Jesus says to the Father: "But now I come to You, and these things I speak [note that He didn't *think* them but *spoke* them] in the world that they may have My joy fulfilled in themselves." Do you remember the prayer of binding and loosing? Doesn't speaking things in the world sound a lot like loosing them, that "they may have My joy fulfilled in themselves"?

5. In verse 15, Jesus frames this in a negative: "I do not pray that You should take them out of the world, but that You should keep them from the evil one." Let's reframe this as a positive: "I pray that You keep them from the evil one."

6. In verse 17, He prays, "Sanctify them by Your truth."

7. In verses 20–21, He said, "I do not pray for these alone, but also for those who will believe in Me through their word; that they all may be one as You, Father, are in Me, and I in You; that they also may be one in Us, that the world may believe that You sent Me."

If you believe in Jesus as a result of reading the Word of God as recorded by His disciples in the Gospels, put your name in the verse so it reads like this: "I do not pray for these alone, but also for [your name here] who has believed in Me through their word."

Jesus then concluded His prayer by declaring His affection for and oneness with the Father.

In this prayer in John 17, Jesus is praying, in essence, for the ministry of His disciples and for all future believers. Notice He stated through faith (v. 20) that some *would believe* in the future, so He again called those things that were not (yet) as though they were.

Thus in this chapter we have seen examples of Jesus praying, using the models of *a petition prayer, a prayer of consecration and dedication, a prayer of intercession,* and possibly *a prayer of binding and loosing.* This is how Jesus prayed.

# Reflections From "How Did Jesus Pray?"

_____

_____

_____

_____

_____

_____

_____

_____

_____

_____

_____

_____

_____

_____

_____

_____

_____

_____

_____

# CHAPTER THREE

# GROUND RULES FOR EFFECTIVE PRAYER

*Be anxious for nothing, but in everything by
prayer and supplication, with thanksgiving,
let your requests be made known to God.*
—PHILIPPIANS 4:6

In our first two chapters, we have seen that there are several types of prayer discussed in the Bible and that each has its own rules. Every situation is not appropriate for each of these prayers, and most of the time only one prayer is appropriate for any particular situation, although they can be used one after another. Then we examined how Jesus prayed and discovered that He taught His disciples, when they needed something, to ask the Father in Jesus's name. They were not to pray to Jesus directly after the Resurrection, and for prayer to "work," the name (or authority) of Jesus had to be invoked. Finally, we examined many reasons why the so-called "Lord's Prayer" really is not a prayer for Christians but was meant as a temporary measure for the disciples while Jesus walked with them.

So the question is, what are the basics of effective prayer? Are there other elements we need—other *mechanisms* that are important to ensure that every prayer is effective? Yes. The Bible has a great deal to say about prayer. In Philippians 4:6, we read this:

> Be anxious for nothing, but in everything by prayer and supplication, with thanksgiving, let your requests be made known to God.

This verse alone is rich with information and instruction about prayer. Let's start at the end, so that I can deal with the following phrase first. Paul says, "Let your requests be made known to God." Doesn't that imply that God doesn't *know* your requests? How can that be? Doesn't God know everything? Yes, He does. And He knows your requests before you request them. Jesus said, "Your heavenly Father knows that you need these things" (Luke 12:30). Obviously, the purpose of making the request for your needs is not for God's benefit—but for yours.

Next, notice that we are to be "anxious for nothing, but in everything by prayer...let your requests be made known to God." Another way to put that would be: "Be anxious for nothing, but pray for everything you need." Nothing...everything. Nothing...everything. There is nothing *left out* of everything. It encompasses all issues that could possibly arise. It addresses all people—men, women, mothers, fathers, children, and so on.

Some people say, "Oh, I don't want to bother God with something that small." (As if asking the Creator of all the universe to be cured of cancer is *big*!) To God, all things are *small*, and yet all things are important or He would not have instructed (this is not a suggestion) to "in everything by prayer . . . let your requests be made known to God." There is nothing too small to bring to God in prayer. If God did not want to be bothered, He had a great opportunity here to tell us!

---

*Humble* means "not arrogant." It does not mean unconfident. It does not mean *un*worthy. In the first place, you cannot come into God's presence—and stay there for any length of time—*if you are unworthy.*

---

Paul does put a *condition* on these requests, namely, that you pray in "supplication, with thanksgiving." Some people think *supplication* means "groveling," but a working definition of *supplication* is simply a "prayer for God's help, or to humbly ask." *Humble* means "not arrogant." It does not mean *un*confident. It does not mean *un*worthy. In the first place, you cannot come into God's presence—and stay there for any length of time—*if you are unworthy.* Satan, because of his prior standing as an angel, could enter the court of almighty God for a few minutes to accuse, because that was his *job*, as it were, to accuse. But he had to leave. Satan could not stay for long in the presence of God—it would literally start to burn him up. So when you bring your requests before God in prayer "and supplication," it means to recognize your place. God is God, and you are His child. Don't get the two mixed up!

## KNOWING WHO YOU ARE IN CHRIST

On the other hand, you must understand who you are in Christ and what rights you have. Look at Hebrews 4:12–16:

> For the word of God is living and powerful, and sharper than any two-edged sword, piercing even to the division of soul and spirit, and of joints and marrow, and is a discerner of the thoughts and intents of the heart. And there is no creature hidden from His sight, but all things are naked and open to the eyes of Him to whom we must give account. Seeing then that we have a great High Priest who has passed through the heavens, Jesus the Son of God, let us hold fast our confession. For we do not have a high priest who cannot sympathize with our weaknesses, but was in all points tempted as we are, yet without sin. Let us therefore come boldly to the throne of grace, that we may obtain mercy and find grace to help in our time of need.

### "Come boldly"

God tells us to "come boldly," that is, without hesitation or timidity. Is it possible to be both *humble* and to *come boldly*? I think so. When my assistant needs to bring something to my attention, she boldly comes into my office and says, "Excuse me, Pastor, but I have a question on this letter." *Excuse me* is, to use Old English wording, "begging favor." She is saying, "Please excuse this interruption," but because she is my assistant and knows that I need to be aware of certain things or approve some documents, she enters right into my office unless I have a "Do Not Disturb" sign up and am in counseling. God didn't just say, "Come to the throne of grace," which would have been enough, but He said, "Come boldly." We have a right to come into the presence of Almighty God.

For what purpose do we "come boldly to the throne of grace?" We come "that we may obtain mercy, and find grace to help in our time of need." Note that it didn't say that we should "come boldly...if it be Thy will." No! That's not boldness. That's really not even humility—it's merely a perceived humility based on ignorance of who you really are in Christ. Even better, this passage in Hebrews says, "Let us therefore come boldly..." It doesn't say, "Let the white folks come boldly," or "Let the black folks come boldly." No! It says, "Let *us*." If you are a born-again believer, you are an *us*, if you get my English!

Think of how long God tried to get the Hebrews to commune with Him, to enter into His presence. But they were afraid of Him: "Then they said to Moses, 'You speak with us, and we will hear; but let not God speak with us, lest we die'" (Exod. 20:19). God never said to the Israelites that they would die if they spoke to Him or He to them. They could not look on His face and live, but that's a different matter. We see the result of their fear in verse 21: "So the people stood afar off, but Moses drew near the thick darkness where God was." God wanted *all* of the Israelites to draw near to Him, but they "stood afar off." After Jesus's resurrection, however, we can draw near to God as He wants—and has always wanted. This is completely consistent with what God has always said, even going back to the Israelites.

## "Pray with thanksgiving"

We are also instructed to pray "with thanksgiving." If you lose sight of what God has given you, you will begin to take Him for granted. Some people pray, "My name is Jimmy; I'll take all you can gimme." Don't forget what He has already done for you. But this has another purpose, which is to keep God's fulfilled promises before your eyes. If you pray in thanksgiving, you constantly repeat—give thanks for—God's blessings in your life. This gives you confidence for what you are asking Him to do for you in the future. Often, Moses would inspire the Israelites by listing all the miraculous things God had already done for them. It's like a coach "firing up" a team before a football game. He might say, "We beat these guys two years ago. We beat them at their place earlier this year. And we've whipped them every time we have played them!"

The players say in their minds, "Yeah. We've beaten them before, and we'll do it again." Thanksgiving serves a twofold purpose: it reminds you of God's goodness, and it gives you confidence for your current (and future) prayers.

## "Make your requests known"

Ultimately, the purpose of coming boldly into God's presence is to "make your requests known" so that God may answer them. I must tell you that I don't have a single unmet need, but I have not always been able to say that. There was a time when my needs had needs, if you know what I mean. Then there was a time when I had a fairly long list of requests. But not anymore! My request list is usually fairly small. Getting to this point, however, took me many years and deliberate practice when it comes to the fundamentals of prayer. It will not come easy for you to reach the same point—there is always a price to be paid. People will misunderstand you and accuse you of all sorts of things, but if you are strong and stay focused on what God has instructed you to do, the criticisms of these people will just roll off you like water off a duck's back.

## PRAY WITH PERSISTENCE

Another aspect of prayer is the need to pray with *persistence.* The King James Bible calls it *importunity.* Some people think that prayer is a form of hounding God. After all, if we are parents, and if we often give in to our kids because they harass us to no end, then maybe the same tactic will work with God. Does God just give us answers to our prayers to get us out of His face? Luke 11:5–8 seems to contradict this.

> And He said to them, "Which of you shall have a friend, and go to him at midnight and say to him, 'Friend, lend me three loaves; for a friend of mine has come to me

on his journey, and I have nothing to set before him';
and he will answer from within, and say, 'Do not trouble me; the door is now shut, and my children are with
me in bed; I cannot rise and give to you'? I say to you,
though he will not rise and give to him because he is his
friend, yet because of his persistence he will rise and give
him as many as he needs.

The New King James translation uses the word *persistence*,
but the King James Version translates this word as *importunity*.
We do not use that word much today, but it means "again and
again and again." Unfortunately, that is the nuance of definition that made it into the New King James with the translation
of the word *persistence*. But another meaning of *importunity* is
"with boldness as though you had a right to be there."

The man in this illustration from Luke 11 was just a friend—
not an employer, not a rabbi—just a friend. Jesus's point was
not that you should hound God until He gives you what you
want. Rather He was teaching us through contrast. If this man
got out of bed in the middle of the night and gave this fellow
bread *just because he was a friend* who had no right to ask for
the food, then imagine how much more we can ask God, *who
through Jesus has given us a right to come into His presence.*

---

God has a proper order for us
to follow, and things will not
work unless we do it His way.

---

Verse 8 says, "I say to you, though he will not rise and give to him because he is his friend, yet because of his persistence [or importunity] he will rise and give him as many as he needs."

## ASK THE *RIGHT* WAY

Jesus then picked up with verses 9–13:

> So I say to you, ask, and it will be given to you; seek, and you will find; knock, and it will be opened to you. For everyone who asks receives, and he who seeks finds, and to him who knocks it will be opened. If a son asks for bread from any father among you, will he give him a stone? Or if he asks for a fish, will he give him a serpent instead of a fish? Or if he asks for an egg, will he offer him a scorpion? If you then, being evil, know how to give good gifts to your children, how much more will your heavenly Father give the Holy Spirit to those who ask Him!

*Asking*, however, requires that we ask in the proper way. As I've already mentioned, there are different types of prayer, and in the case of petition prayer, we have already been told by Jesus to ask the Father in the name of Jesus. So that is our model.

When I was in elementary school, I learned a lesson about asking for things in the proper way. One day in class the teacher gave us an assignment. She said if we completed the assignment and turned in our paper before the bell for recess rang, we would be allowed to go out to the play yard early.

One by one, students completed the assignment and left the room. When I had finished, I put my pencil in the little box, handed my paper to the teacher, and said, "Can I go out and play now?" I was sincere in my question, but I was sincerely wrong in the way I phrased my question. When I asked, "Can I go out and play?" she replied, "I don't know. *Can* you?" I didn't understand what she was getting at, so I asked the same thing. "Teacher, I finished my paper. Can I go out and play?" Again she said, "*Can* you?" By that time I was really getting frustrated. I said, "Look, I put my paper in the stack, I put my pencil in the box, and now I want to know, can I go outside and play?" Again, she said, "*Can* you?" She saw I was not getting it, so she explained to me that I was asking if I had the ability to go outside and play—which of course I did. But I needed to ask, "*May* I go outside?" because I needed the *permission* to go outside.

Through Jesus, we have been given the *permission* (or authority) to expect answered prayer and the *ability* to conduct God's operations in this world, but if you stand there asking for the ability when you already have it, you are essentially calling God a liar. He has said you have it; you are saying you don't. This is the point: God has a proper order for us to follow, and things will not work unless we do it His way.

> If an unjust judge will dispense justice
> to the woman to shut her up, think
> of how much more we, as children of
> a loving God, can expect to receive
> from Him when we have been invited
> to come and speak with Him.

For a moment, let's return to this notion of persistence, because Luke 18:1–8 has a second passage that is often misused in the context of prayer:

Then He spoke a parable to them, that men always ought to pray and not lose heart, saying, "There was in a certain city a judge who did not fear God nor regard man. Now there was a widow in that city; and she came to him, saying, 'Get justice for me from my adversary.' And he would not for a while; but afterward he said within himself, 'Though I do not fear God nor regard man, yet because this widow troubles me I will avenge her, lest by her continual coming she weary me.'" Then the Lord said, "Hear what the unjust judge said. And shall God not avenge His own elect who cry out day and night to Him, though He bears long with them? I tell you that He will avenge them speedily. Nevertheless, when the Son of Man comes, will He really find faith on the earth?"

In this passage, we again see a person—a widow, in this case—who is persistent. The judge saw that by her "continual coming," she would wear him out, so he gave her what she wanted. While this isn't specifically about prayer, it is connected to prayer by many ministers who argue that you need to be persistent with God. By that, they mean you have to (in slang English) "bug" God until He finally relents and gives you what you want.

That is *not* the message of this passage in Luke, anymore than it was the message of the earlier passage in Luke. Did you notice that the "judge" was a man who "did not fear God nor regard man?" This can't possibly describe the Father, who is just. This judge didn't care about the woman. He only agrees to give her justice so that he can get rid of her. Jesus's point, again, is *contrast*: If an unjust judge will dispense justice to the woman to shut her up, think of how much more we, as children of a loving God, can expect to receive from Him when we have been invited to come and speak with Him.

Moreover, you cannot *make* God do anything. Do you really think that by nagging the Creator of the universe you can browbeat Him into doing something He doesn't really want to do? If God is eternal, can your repeated crabbing—even if you do it ten times a day, every day of your life—influence a Being who has been around since before time began? Do you think God can't outlast you?

So we are back to Jesus's instructions in Luke 11:9 to "ask," "seek," and "knock." Jesus said: "Ask, and it will be given to you; seek, and you will find; knock, and it will be opened to you." Note what Jesus *did not say!* Did you read any conditions at all on those instructions? Did Jesus say, "Ask, and if it is the Father's will, it will be given to you," or "Seek, and if God wants you to find it, you will find it"? No. There were no conditions. Of course you realize that God cannot sin, and therefore He will not participate in your sin. So you cannot ask God, for example, to line you up with a prostitute or help you cheat your boss and expect an answer to that prayer. That will not happen. Jesus clearly means that as long as you ask in line with what God has said, it will be given you.

---

God's grace and His promises
are available to everyone. He is
an *equal opportunity blesser!*

---

Then He said, "For everyone who asks receives, and he who seeks finds, and to him who knocks it will be opened" (v. 10). That is pretty powerful! *Who* would receive or find or have it opened? *Everyone.* For minorities in this and other countries who have experienced discrimination, that is good news. Jesus didn't say, "For all the white people who ask," or " For all the Jews who ask," or "For all people living in Hollywood who ask." No! He said *everyone.* God's grace and His promises are available to everyone. He is an *equal opportunity blesser!*

## Have Faith for What You Ask For

Let's continue on with verses 11–13:

> If a son asks for bread from any father among you, will he give him a stone? Or if he asks for a fish, will he give him a serpent instead of a fish? Or if he asks for an egg, will he offer him a scorpion? If you then, being evil, know how to give good gifts to your children, how much more will your heavenly Father give the Holy Spirit to those who ask Him!

I've been in several denominations where I was told, "Brother Price, you have to be prepared, because the Lord knows what's best for you. Sometimes God in His wisdom and mercy will give you what you asked for, and sometimes He knows that if you get what you asked for that you might become swollen with pride or get caught up in the thing and stop coming to church. So God knows that it was better for you to have this rather than what you asked for." Jesus told us that we should ask the Father for the things we want. If God knows already, and knows He isn't going to give it to us, why bother?

I submit to you that you should get what you ask for—as long as it's in line with the Word—and if you don't, you didn't get an answered prayer. If you just pray for a car, then be prepared to get some piece of junk with one wheel falling off. God has indeed answered your prayer. But if you pray, "Lord, I need a new SUV that will carry all my equipment plus the kids' stuff for all of their athletic events," and you instead get a compact car, then God did not answer that prayer.

---

**Don't wait until you get a diagnosis of cancer to "start believing" in healing. Begin believing for healing with maladies that are not life threatening, like headaches or upset stomachs.**

---

At this point, however, I need to add one important qualification. If you pray for a Rolls Royce, you better have Rolls Royce faith. It's important to understand that God's power to provide your prayer requests never changes, but your faith can. Remember that in Nazareth, we found that Jesus could do no mighty works because of the people's unbelief. Jesus, the Son of God! The same Jesus who walked on water, raised the dead, and healed the lepers. But in Nazareth did He suddenly lose His power? No! What changed was that in other examples of Jesus's power at work, especially healing, Jesus's power was mixed with the individual's faith. Even at Lazarus's tomb, maybe Lazarus couldn't help much (because he was dead!), but the women could believe Lazarus would rise again—and they did. And on the Sea of Galilee when the disciples woke Jesus up and said, in so many words, "Lord, man, you gotta help us! We're about to sink!" it was their faith that He could save them that became a conduit for Jesus to save them.

We know that there are levels of faith, because Jesus spoke of "great faith" (Matt. 8:10) and "little" faith (Matt. 6:30). Both groups of people had faith, but some had more faith than others. Romans 12:3 says that we all have been given "a measure of faith." The King James Version says we have all been given "the measure of faith," meaning we all start out with the same amount of faith. Peter had enough faith to get out of a perfectly good boat and walk on water—for a little while. But he didn't have enough faith to ignore the wind and the storm. Doubt is the enemy of faith, and sometimes you can have more faith—for example, before you begin to think about something—than you have later if you begin mulling over in your mind all the reasons why something "won't work."

A faith-filled believer who worked in an office situation had an emergency arise where he needed to copy some documents right away. But when he got to the copy room, three or four people were standing around looking at the copier. They told him that it was broken and they didn't know what was wrong with it. The power was off, and they just couldn't fix it. At that point, he had no other choice but to use his faith—and no time to worry about what people would say—so he walked up to the copier, laid hands on it, and said in a loud voice, "In the name of Jesus, I command you to work."

That copier hummed to life and made his copies, then promptly shut back down as the next person came up to use it! He told me that if he had tried to prepare for that situation by thinking about it, his natural mind would have told him he couldn't do that, and it wouldn't have worked. Yet it worked because *at that moment* he had no doubt whatsover. I believe the same was true for Peter: at the moment he stepped out of that boat, he had no doubt whatsoever he could walk on water. It was only after his mind started telling him that what he was doing was impossible that he began to sink.

Prayer depends, in part, on your faith. When I was first starting out in faith, we bought a car for $151 a month. That car payment was bigger than our house payment. It took everything we had to believe for that $151 a month. But as we have grown in faith, our ability to believe for bigger things has grown. Since that time, I've bought two cars for my wife that cost $60,000 apiece and paid cash for them. Here's the point: we didn't start there, but you have to start somewhere. It's the same thing with healing. Don't wait until you get a diagnosis of cancer to "start believing" in healing. You'll be dead as a doorknob if you do! No, begin believing for healing with maladies that are not life threatening, like headaches or upset stomachs.

---

The *what* that you pray for is merely your *direction* in prayer. But the *means* to unleash God's power is *faith*.

---

Realize that the devil has a vested interest in trying to make sure you do *not* get your prayers answered. He will even attempt to "answer" your prayers with something other than—less

91

than—what you asked for. As an example, say you prayed for an SUV, but someone came along and said, "God told me to give you this Volkswagen." Nothing against the Volkswagen, but it was not what you prayed for. If you accept that *as* the answer to your prayer, then you have accepted defeat. There would be nothing wrong if you accepted it, sold the car, and applied the money to the car you prayed for, but if you do not get what you pray for, your prayer was not answered.

## You Must Believe ... to Receive

This brings us to the essence of the prayer of faith, or petition prayer. Prayer has incredible power because it acts as a release mechanism. Think of it this way: You have a giant electric generator in a factory. Every morning the workman goes in and flips a switch, and that huge dynamo comes to life, unleashing enormous power. Would you seriously claim that the power was "in" the switch? No, but without switching on that power, that generator just sits there. Your prayer is a switch, allowing the power of God to flow into your life and through you. The question we want to answer is, "How do I flip that switch?"

We have looked at some of these principles for "flipping the switch" already, but the most succinct and direct instructions by Jesus on how to pray in faith are found in Mark 11:24. This comes at the end of a short lesson on using your faith to move mountains. In verse 24, Jesus said:

Therefore I say to you, whatever things you ask when you pray, believe that you receive them, and you will have them.

You would be surprised at how many people read that verse and think they read something else. What did Jesus say you would receive when you pray? He did *not* say you would receive "what you asked for." He placed a condition on that by saying, "Whatever thing you ask when you pray, *believe that you receive them*, and you will have them." What does the "them" refer to? It refers to those things you really believed *you would receive when you prayed*. You might want something very badly, and you might ask for it in prayer, but if you really did not believe you received it, guess what? You will not get it! It seems like a small point, but it makes all the difference in the world. The *what* that you pray for is merely your *direction* in prayer. But the *means* to unleash God's power is *faith*, or believing that you receive *when* you pray. Matthew recorded this slightly differently: "And whatever things you ask in prayer, believing, you will receive" (Matt. 21:22).

---

## The greater your faith, the sooner you can receive answers to prayer.

---

It's amazing that in the natural world, we have no problem with the way things work. We go through certain protocols because "that's the way it is." If a weedwhacker or snowblower says, "Push button five times before starting," we do that automatically. Sometimes we'll try five or six, but very few people will say, "I'm not doing that. What's the purpose of that?" In the natural, of course, the purpose is to prime the engine so it has fuel when you want to start it. For those people who live in snowy climates, if you get in a skid, the driving instructors tell you to turn into the skid. Huh? That doesn't sound right. But anyone with any sense knows that's how you straighten out your car. For hundreds of years, man tried to fly by flapping wings or pushing *against* air, until finally some people found that you can lift something that is heavier than air by creating a wing shape that causes lift. But be honest: how many of you *really* understand the principles of aerodynamics, so that when you see a 747 go up, you can say, "Sure, I understand that"? Yet most of you don't have a problem flying and just accepting that *something* is making that airplane go into the sky.

Yet when it comes to the things of God, we have great difficulty accepting God's method of doing things—His instruction manual. Jesus said, "Whatever things you ask when you pray, believe that you receive them, and you will have them." The key, then, is that at the moment you pray, you must believe that you receive. Not after you pray, and not even before you pray. *Present tense.* That faith is the triggering device—it's the wing shape that gives your prayer lift; it's the pump priming that causes your prayer engine to start up. Again, I have to be clear here: *what* you believe is critical. It's not just that you believe God is God, or that Jesus is His Son. Those are prerequisites, but at the moment you pray for something, you must believe you receive it. Jesus said, "Believe that you receive them, and you will have them." Did you catch that? Your *believing* is present tense, but your receiving ("will have") is *future* tense.

"How soon will I receive what I prayed for?" you might ask. That will be dependent on several things. First, how rapidly something comes into physical reality depends on your faith, as I have written earlier. The greater your faith, the sooner you can receive answers to prayer. Related to that, a second factor that determines how long you must wait for answers to prayer in the natural (and I keep phrasing this way because that prayer has already been answered in the spiritual realm) is the nature or size of your prayer request. Money, for example, doesn't just fall out of the sky; other people must bring it into your hands. So, say you prayed for a certain large bill to be paid. At that moment God answered your prayer, and perhaps He did so by directing someone to send you a check in the mail. Although that check hasn't actually arrived yet, it *is* a reality. The check has been written, mailed, and is on its way to you.

There is another factor that determines how quickly you actually see in the natural the answer to your prayer. We have an enemy, the devil. One of the devil's jobs is to shake our faith, and one of the best ways to shake our faith is to attack our patience. As humans, we aren't very patient. Watch people after a stoplight turns green, and see how quickly they honk their horns if the person in front of them doesn't move instantly. (A humorist once wrote that the smallest time frame known to man is the time between a New York streetlight turning green and the cabbie behind you hitting his horn!)

Satan knows we have little patience, that we live in a "now" society. He knows that if he can just delay an answered prayer, even for a few days, some people will stop believing—and once that happens, it's as if the prayer had never been answered in the first place. Often, then, the devil or his demons will intercept prayer answers and detour them, delay them, hold them up somehow hoping you will get off your confession of faith.

*In the interim between your prayer and the physical manifestation of your healing, don't talk about the symptoms. Address the solution. It's important not to get caught up in talking about feelings.*

In Daniel chapters 9–10, we see Daniel praying, asking for mercy for the Israelites (supplication), but also needing the ability to interpret dreams. In Daniel 10:12, Daniel was visited by an angel, who said, "From the first day that you set your heart to understand, and to humble yourself before your God, your words were heard; and I have come because of your words." Note right there that God answered Daniel's prayer, not after several days, but on the "first day." Also note that it was Daniel's words that set everything in motion—the angel came because of Daniel's words!

But then look at what it says in verse 13: "But the prince of the kingdom of Persia withstood me twenty-one days; and behold, Michael, one of the chief princes, came to help me, for I had been left alone there with the kings of Persia." Friend, if this were a battle between an angel and an earthly prince, it would be no contest. There is no man who has ever been born who could defeat an angel in combat. The phrases "prince of the kingdom of Persia" and "Michael, one of the chief princes" both indicate that angelic beings are referred to in the Bible as "princes." What happened was that God answered Daniel's prayer immediately and sent an angel to carry out the assignment, but the demonic spirit known as the "prince of Persia" intercepted the angel and fought with him for three earthly weeks, until finally Michael arrived, and the two of them drove off this demonic spirit.

That gap of time between when you ask—believing that you receive—and the physical manifestation of your prayer request is then subject to: (1) your faith, (2) the nature or size of the request relative to your faith, and (3) the resistance of the devil. Look at what Daniel did in the interim: "In those days I, Daniel, was mourning three full weeks" (Dan. 10:2). He mourned over the state of Jerusalem and was interceding for the Israelites. He did not beg God and every day say, "Lord, why haven't You answered my prayer?" Instead, he focused on praying for others.

This brings me to an important point. If you pray and believe that you receive something, and yet the next day you ask for it again, then you really didn't believe you received it the first time. You can only pray a petition prayer, as such, one time, or you are not following Jesus's instructions: "When you pray, believe that you receive them [the things you ask for], and you will have them." By asking for something again, you demonstrate that you really did not believe that you had it in the first place. If you believed, you would not have asked again.

What do you do in the interim—the time between when you ask for something in prayer and the time that you physically receive it—if you can only ask for something once? You *thank* God for what He has already delivered to you. "Father, thank You. I believe I receive that new washer that we need." When it comes to healing, you need to say, "Father, I thank You. I believe that I am healed."

People get hung up on this confession. Some people feel that if they don't *talk the problem*, others will think they are lying. For example, if you are waiting for the physical manifestation of your healing from a tumor, you cannot say that tumor isn't there. If your blood sugar is low, you can't say it isn't. But in the interim between your prayer and the physical manifestation of your healing, you just do *not have to talk about it—you do not have to talk about the symptoms.* If someone asks, "How are you?" or "How are you feeling?" you just say, "Well, based on God's Word I believe I'm healed." Instead of talking about the *symptoms*, you address the *solution*. It's important not to get caught up in talking about *feelings*: "For we walk by faith, not by sight [or feelings]" (2 Cor. 5:7).

We do this all the time in the natural, and no one has a bit of trouble with it. A woman, for example, might have a friend who is seriously overweight—can we be blunt?—fat! And yet we say (honestly) to her, "Your hair looks so good," or "You have the most beautiful skin." Professionals from business leaders to teachers learn to focus on the positive in someone. You'll hear them say to an employee, "You have such energy!" Or to a student, "Johnny, that was a wonderful essay you wrote." Normally, you won't hear them say to the employee, "You have bad breath," or to the student, "... but your math grade is pitiful!"

This is the secret: refusing to talk about the problem continually is not *lying* about whether you have the problem. You cannot deny an X-ray, or a mortgage-in-arrears notice. And by all means, I am not saying that you refuse to discuss things with professionals, such as doctors, lawyers, accountants, or with spouses or family members when it comes to planning a strategy in the natural to deal with a problem. Remember, we are fighting a war on two fronts—the physical and the spiritual. In the natural world, you might need to get medical help, have an operation, or take medicine. You may need to get financial help, refinance your house, or do whatever it takes. To state the facts to a doctor or accountant is not "unbelief." What you say is, "I see that tumor, doctor. Let's attack that aggressively in the natural, but in the meantime, I believe God has already dealt with that tumor in the spirit realm."

We seem to have no problem with this process in the natural world. You will say, "I can go to the basketball game with you Saturday, because I get paid on Friday." In fact, you don't really know that you will get paid on Friday—you believe it. Every time you say that, you are really making a faith confession, except in this case you apparently have more faith in your employer than you do in God.

Early in my faith walk, I had a test in this respect. Many years ago as a young teen, while showering, I felt a small lump underneath the mammary gland, about the size of a green pea, in the left side of my chest cavity. I paid little attention to it at first, but as time passed it grew to the size of a quarter and became very painful to the touch. Shortly after high school I married. At that time the pain was unbearable. I went to the doctor and had it examined. The doctor said I had a tumor or growth. He couldn't say if it was cancerous or benign. He said it needed to be removed surgically if I was to get any relief from it.

After the operation the doctor informed me that it was not cancerous; however, vestiges of this kind of growth could possibly float over to the right side of the chest cavity and begin to grow there. Many years later, as the doctor had warned, while showering I noticed a small pea-sized growth under the mammary gland in the right side of my chest cavity. Unlike the first growth, which grew very slowly, this one seemed to spring up overnight and became extremely painful.

---

If the devil can get you into the arena of feelings and sight instead of in the arena of faith, he will take you out.

---

But this time I had come into the knowledge of faith and healing. I took my stand on Mark 11:24, Matthew 8:17, and 1 Peter 2:24. I said, "Father, You said in Your Word, Matthew 8:17, referring to Jesus, 'He Himself took our infirmities and bore our sicknesses.' And in 1 Peter 2:24, again referring to Jesus, You said, 'By whose stripes you were healed.' In Mark 11:24, Jesus said, 'Therefore I say unto you, what things soever ye desire, when ye pray, believe that ye receive them, and ye shall have them (KJV).' I am now praying, and I say, 'Father, I desire that this tumor or growth be healed. According to Your Word, I believe that I receive my healing now, in Jesus's name. Thank You, Father. I believe I am healed.'" From that point on, the battle was on. As time went on the tumor grew larger and hurt worse. Every day in my prayer time, I reminded the Father, "I believe that I am healed." You have to keep your confession in the present tense.

This went on for months. In the natural, every day the first thing that would come to my mind was a thought from the devil. "Fred, how do you feel?"

I would say, "Devil, I do not walk by how I feel. I walk by faith and not by sight. According to the Word of God, with Jesus's stripes, I was healed, and if I was, then I am, and if I am, then '*I is*,' because Hebrews 11:1 says: 'Now faith is...,' and I believe I am healed." If the devil can get you into the arena of feelings and sight, instead of in the arena of faith, he will take you out.

In my case, I continued praying for many months, "Father, I thank You. I believe I'm healed." Finally, eleven months had passed, and one day I was in the shower, just soaping up, and all of a sudden, I noticed I didn't feel the pain. I stopped, grabbed my chest, and lo and behold, the tumor was gone. Vanished. At that point, I prayed a different prayer: "Father, I thank You. I am healed." I no longer had to believe it as a faith fact, because now I had it as a physical fact.

## Reflections From "Ground Rules for Effective Prayer"

_____

_____

_____

_____

_____

_____

_____

_____

_____

_____

_____

_____

_____

_____

# Reflections From "Ground Rules for Effective Prayer"

_____

_____

_____

_____

_____

_____

_____

_____

_____

_____

_____

_____

# CHAPTER FOUR

# WHAT TO PRAY FOR

*God knows that if you truly are in tune with
His Word, you will never ask for something
sinful.... That is what allows Him to make
the blanket promise in 1 John that if we
ask anything according to His will, He not
only hears us, but we have assurance that
because He hears us, we have our petitions.*

## STEP 1: DETERMINE WHAT YOU WANT

We had to review some basics about prayer before we get to the actual formula that we need to use for an answered prayer, but here it is.

Step one is to determine what it is we want, then find the promises for that in God's Word. *What* we are entitled to pray for is anything that God has promised us. Your Bible is the inventory list. We have what's called the New Covenant, which lists everything we would ever need or desire that is consistent with a godly life. This really is the first step in the "how to pray" process, but for some reason, next to believing we receive when we pray, this is the toughest step. It's hard because the Bible doesn't state explicitly every single thing we need or desire. But God does give us examples of what we are entitled to through our New Covenant, so our study of the Word requires that we apply our reason to determine, "Does this thing fit in this category?" Nevertheless, the Bible covers every single issue of life that we could face. All we have to do is to find out what the Bible promises on a certain subject.

For example, what does God say about healing in His Word? Healing is one of the things that I am entitled to pray for based on the Word of God. In Matthew 8:16–17, we read:

> When evening had come, they brought to Him many who were demon-possessed. And He cast out the spirits with a word, and healed all who were sick that it might be fulfilled which was spoken by Isaiah the prophet, saying, "He Himself took our infirmities and bore our sicknesses."

In 1 Peter 2:24, the Bible tells me: "... by whose stripes you were healed." As far as God is concerned, if I was sick at any time, now I "were" healed, if you will pardon my grammar. God has said, "He Himself [Jesus] took our infirmities and bore our sicknesses," and that I was healed by His stripes. But remember, in *God's time frame* there is no past. So if I have been healed, then I *am healed*.

When we begin to search the Bible for those things that we are authorized to pray for, it is worth remembering that the Bible is the "last will and testament" of the Lord Jesus Christ—that, in fact, is why they call it the *New Testament*. A testament is a will, or a statement of the deceased's desires regarding the disposition of his property. Except in our case, our Trustee is still alive—Jesus—but He has gone to the next world, leaving us with His intentions in this one.

---

God hears you in the now, and He meets your need in the now, but depending on your level of faith, the size of the need, and the opposition of the enemy, you may not physically see it or touch it until the future.

---

Go back to the verse I referenced earlier, 1 John 5:14: "Now this is the confidence that we have in Him, that if we ask anything according to His will, He hears us." So we know that if we are asking in His will, God hears us. But it gets even better in verse 15: "And if we know that He hears us, whatever we ask, we know that we have the petitions that we have asked of Him." Does "whatever we ask" sound like Mark 11:24? "Whatever things you ask when you pray, believe that you receive them, and you will have them." It most certainly does. The key in each case is that the *anything* we ask must be "according to His will." But once we are in that groove, if you will, we can go *anywhere* with our prayer requests, and we will have the answer to our petitions—keeping in mind that prayer requires faith and that there is an opponent who will delay our prayer requests being fulfilled, but who cannot stop them.

## YOUR ASKING MUST BE *PRESENT TENSE*

John's words in 1 John 5:14–15 mimic Jesus's earlier words in Mark 11. John tells us, "If we ask anything according to His will, He *hears* us" (present tense), and "...whatever we ask, we *know* [present tense] that *we have* [present tense] the petitions that *we have asked* [past tense] of Him" (emphasis added). This is such an amazing truth if we can only grasp on to it. Our *asking* is present tense. The time that we *ask* for something is right now, whatever time that is. At that point, God *hears* us. He hears us *in the present.*

When describing our prayer, we will say that we *asked* (past tense) for something, but we *know* (present tense) we *have* (present tense) the things we *asked* (past tense) for. Here is where it is tricky: When you *ask*, you must *believe*. You *know* because you believe, and in the past your belief has produced evidence that what you now request you *have* now, even if you won't *physically see it or be able to touch it until the future.* I need to reiterate this point one more time. The believing must be in the *now*, the same time as the asking. God hears you in the now, and He meets your need in the now, but depending on your level of faith, the size of the need, and the opposition of the enemy, you may not physically see it or touch it until the future.

These are not word games, but rather this is the essence of successful prayer.

When you pray for something, you must know that whatever you ask for is *godly*. How do you know that? You know by checking it out in His Word. Has He promised this to you or to your spiritual ancestors, the Jews, through Abraham, Isaac, Jacob, and the rest? If they were entitled to it, and if it was not specific to them (i.e., occupying the Holy Land), then all who are of "Abraham's seed" are entitled to any of those promises, *plus* all the promises of Jesus. God knows that if you truly are in tune with His Word, you will never ask for something sinful or stupid or ungodly. That is what allows Him to make the blanket promise in 1 John that if we ask *anything* according to His will, not only does He hear us, but also we have assurance that because He hears us, we have our petitions.

John says, "Now this is the confidence that we have in Him." What is confidence? It is trust, right? If I have confidence in you, it means I can trust you. This is the "trust that we have in Him." We can trust God that when we pray, He hears us and has answered our petition. That is a fact. In John 11, Jesus said, "Father, I thank You that You have heard Me." He didn't say, "Father, I hope You heard Me, and, Father, if it be Thy will..." No! Jesus *knew* it was the Father's will, and that is why He *knew that God heard Him!*

Do you see how this takes all the guesswork out of prayer? Can you see why people who don't understand this accuse me of being "arrogant"? "Well, who does he think he is that God always hears his prayers?" That's easy: I am a child of God in

109

the way I hope that you are a child of God, and I ask according to His Word. I don't ask anything that is not according to His Word, so I am 100 percent assured that He hears me every time I pray.

By listening to the prayers that people pray in many churches, you can hear that they have failed to focus their prayers on the Word of God. Instead, many prayers are focused on sounding "spiritual" or quoting Bible verses.

## PRAY ACCORDING TO THE WORD OF GOD

We have already discussed why the so-called "Lord's Prayer" may not be appropriate for Christians today, but if it were, wouldn't you say that it was formulaic? After all, you'd be saying the same thing almost every time. The same is true of our petition prayers today. If you are praying in line with the Word and, for example, you are asking for healing, then your prayer is going to be based on the same few scriptures every time.

> *Father, today I ask that You heal me of this stomach condition. Your Word says in 1 Peter 2:24 that by His stripes I was healed. In Isaiah Your Word says that Jesus has borne our griefs and carried our sorrows. Therefore, Lord, I thank You that according to Your Word I have the promise that I am healed.*

Knowing the specific scriptures to include in your prayers requires some work by you. You must go through the Bible and find out what has been promised to the Jews specifically (i.e., what would not apply to you as a modern American). Then find out what has been promised to Abraham's seed (that is, the Jews and those who inherited the promises made to the Jews, which would be Christians). Finally, find out those things that are promised to Christians specifically.

As an illustration, earlier I suggested that you read Deuteronomy 28. One-third of that chapter contains blessings for those who are obedient to God. This portion of Scripture was not directed at the Jews only but included those who were the descendants of the Jews. We find there:

> And all these blessings shall come upon you and overtake you, because you obey the voice of the LORD your God: Blessed shall you be in the city, and blessed shall you be in the country. Blessed shall be the fruit of your body [your children], the produce of your ground and the increase of your herds, the increase of your cattle and the offspring of your flocks.
>
> —DEUTERONOMY 28:2–4

There were no special qualifications for obtaining these blessings other than obedience to the Lord. Based on these verses, you know that it is God's will for you to be blessed whether you live in the city or in a rural area. Your children should also be blessed and therefore should not suffer from diseases like ADD, SIDs, or any other disease. Moreover, while today we don't farm and therefore don't have lots of "ground" or "herds" or "cattle" or "flocks," that doesn't mean we don't have claim to this promise. Ground and herds and flocks were merely the way most people made a living in that time.

Today our equivalent would be to say "in your *factories*, in your *investment houses*, in your *work*, and in your *job*." Cattle and flocks were currency in those days—they were stores of wealth. So it's fully legitimate to substitute, "... the produce of your investment and retirement accounts and the increase of your bank and checking accounts and the multiplication of your finances."

---

> You have a right to pray for healing
> and for prosperity, as well as for
> the health of your children and
> for victory over your enemies.

---

We can make the same conclusions in verse 5, which says, "Blessed shall be your basket and your kneading bowl." People kept their grain in baskets and made it into bread in kneading bowls. This verse is saying that we should be blessed in our financial dealings when we turn raw materials or labor into profits. Verse 6 echoes verse 3: "Blessed shall you be when you come in, and blessed shall you be when you go out." That pretty much covers everything you do, because you would be blessed all the time, everywhere.

Verse 7 continues by saying, "The LORD will cause your enemies who rise against you to be defeated before your face; they shall come out against you one way and flee before you seven ways." This is true for individuals as well as for nations

112

whose hearts are directed toward God. On an individual basis, the Bible is telling you that you will have enemies and that they will rise against you. You won't get away from that. But they will be "defeated before your face." So it is fully legitimate to pray for your enemies' defeat—and this implies that you will have a hand in that defeat. The verse does not say that God will kill them before they even get to you—in fact, the verse indicates they will get in your face. You must be the one who defeats them, but *they will be defeated.* The Bible even indicates that you will witness their defeat as they "come out against you one way and flee before you seven ways."

In verse 8, it is written: "The LORD will command the blessing on you in your storehouses and in all to which you set your hand, and He will bless you in the land which the LORD your God is giving you." In Abraham's times, farmers had storehouses where they kept their surplus. Today we also have storehouses where we *store* our surplus for later or to sell. Our storehouses are our bank accounts, our stock and bond portfolios, and our IRA/Keough accounts. This verse tells me that God will "command the blessing" on you. That's pretty powerful stuff, to command a blessing on your storehouses.

There is much, much more, but you get the idea. From just a few verses in Deuteronomy and 1 Peter, we have discovered that you have a right to pray for healing and for prosperity, as well as for the health of your children and for victory over your enemies. Imagine how much more is promised to you in the rest of the Bible! However, you must expend the effort to find it. Once you find it on your own, you will never forget it, and, more importantly, you will never doubt that it is God's will. And you will know specifically the blessings of God for which you should be praying. You should never, ever, tack "if it be Your will" onto the end of a petition prayer. By doing so you are indicating that, in fact, you do not know God's will. John said that if we pray *according to His will*, our prayers are answered.

---

**If you have identified something that, without a doubt, is promised to you by Scripture—such as healing or prosperity—then *no* is *not an answer from God*.**

---

It would be impossible for me to list everything you would be legitimately allowed to pray for according to God's Word, because I cannot envision every situation that might come up in your life. Even if I gave you general guidelines for praying about money, or relationships, or whatever the case, it would defeat the purpose—in that *you* need to find it so that you know what is in the Word.

However, let me give you just one more example of what you may legitimately claim. Psalm 91:10 says, "No evil shall befall you, nor shall any plague come near your dwelling." Here is the *catch*. If you don't know that verse, you cannot confess what you don't know, and you will be unable to use the blessings of the Word to be protected from any "plague" (like the bird flu, for example) coming near your dwelling. Hosea 4:6 quotes God as saying, "My people are destroyed for lack of knowledge." Note that God did not say, "My people are destroyed for lack of *faith*," or even "My people are destroyed for lack of *love*." If you have the knowledge, you at least know how to build your faith and to develop more of a loving spirit, but without the knowledge, you are history!

Here is your assignment: go through the New Testament (we'll limit it to the New Testament for now) and underline every time you find the phrase "You have" or "we have" when it relates to the phrase "in Christ." What do we have, or what do you have, in Christ? You will be shocked to see how much we are promised. Psalm 84:11 said of God, "No good thing will He withhold from those who walk uprightly." James said, "Every good and perfect gift is from above, and comes down from the Father of lights" (James 1:17).

In the Epistles of John we have a clear example of prayer that lists some of the blessings to which we are entitled. In 3 John 2, in a letter addressed to a fellow Christian and elder named Gaius, John said:

> Beloved, I pray that you may prosper in all things and be in health, just as your soul prospers.

The apostle of the Lord was telling Gaius, a fellow believer, that his prayer for him was that he "prosper in all *things*." And to make sure we didn't miss his meaning, John wrote, "just as your soul prospers," indicating that he was praying for "things" apart from the spirit world. Some people try to claim that by "things," John meant *spiritual things*, but it is abundantly clear by this verse that this isn't the case. Note that John also prayed for Gaius's health. So if it was all right for John to pray for Gaius's prosperity, for Gaius's health, and for Gaius's soul to prosper, don't you think *Gaius could also legitimately pray for those things for himself?* I do, and I'm sure Gaius did.

## NO IS NOT AN ANSWER FROM GOD

Decide what you want from God, then find out if Scripture promises you that. Let me be absolutely clear on this: if you have identified something that, without a doubt, is promised to you by Scripture—such as healing or prosperity—then *no* is *not an answer from God.* In 2 Corinthians 1:20, Paul wrote: "For all the promises of God in Him [Jesus] are Yes, and in Him Amen." How many promises are left out of "all?" None, right?

Do not be fooled by teachers who tell you, "Sometimes God says yes; sometimes God says no; and sometimes God says wait." The verse you just read in 2 Corinthians proves that if the question is *godly*, the answer can never, ever be no. Since God is only in the eternal present and does not have a past or future, neither can He say wait. There is only *now* for God. But there are reasons why what you possess immediately in the spirit world has not immediately been manifested in the physical world. Those reasons include your level of faith, the nature of the thing believed for, and the level of demonic opposition.

If you have allowed a tumor to grow in your body for five years and just now want to get rid of it, it isn't God saying wait on healing. It took five years to get there, so it won't disappear instantly. It isn't God saying wait on getting your debts paid if it took you twenty years to pile up $50,000 worth of debt. Like a bolt that is removed by using a torque wrench, the moment you start applying your faith to your need in prayer, immediately the answer is already breaking free—you just can't feel it yet. At some point, the whole thing gives, and the answer seems to manifest instantly. But it really did not happen *overnight*. Rather, you have been applying steady faith pressure to the issue through your confession and prayer.

## BE DEFINITE IN YOUR PRAYER

There is another aspect to your prayer. You have to be definite. Gloria Copeland has a great line regarding this. She says, "If you want the dog, don't call the cat." You must be specific about what is promised to you in the Bible. If the promise is there, you are completely within your rights to ask for it in faith. How it is actually delivered, however, is usually through the hands of man. In Joshua 1:8, God tells Joshua: "For then you will make your way prosperous...." God did not say *He* would—even though the verses we read in Deuteronomy show that He indeed will. He said, "*You* will."

117

Aside from the manna falling from heaven, God has never just dropped blessings on people. His blessings have always come through the hands of man. The blessings that He reveals in Deuteronomy are, for the most part, blessings that require your involvement, such as farming or working or "kneading." Jesus could have just taken thin air and fed all the hungry people on the mountainside, but He asked for the loaves and the fishes and multiplied them. How does money come into your *storehouses*? It comes through money, salaries, and checks that people write to you.

We are not just leaves blown in the wind. We have something to do with our destinies. That is the whole point of the Law—"Thou shalt/Thou shalt not." It acknowledges that we have a role to play in the natural in getting our prayers answered. Contrary to what some people think, the phrase "God helps those who help themselves" is not in the Bible. But it does express a principle: in the natural, and in faith, you must do those things that reflect that you believe you have received your prayer request.

---

## If God has called you to do something, He will strengthen you to do it.

---

In Matthew 4:7, Jesus said, "You shall not tempt the LORD your God." If you do not do in the natural what you should be doing, merely asking God to answer your need, in essence, you are tempting God. For example, if you pray to be delivered from debt, then quit your job that same day, you are tempting God. Nor would it be an act of faith to say, "Lord, please deliver me from debt," and then refuse to accept your employer's offer of six months' worth of overtime.

In other words, unless you have specific instructions from God otherwise, you need to do in the natural the things that are consistent with achieving your prayer request. Here is another example: you cannot pray for healing of cancer, then go home and say, "Well, God has that under control, so I'm going to start smoking and using drugs." Sorry, that's not faith; that's presumption, and it is tempting God.

There is a common "preacher joke" that makes a very important point in this regard, and it's especially relevant in light of the flooding in New Orleans after Katrina. There was a flood headed for a little town, and the sheriff's cruiser came through town blaring orders over the loudspeaker to evacuate. One man walked out on his porch and said, "God will provide." Several hours later, everyone else had evacuated, but the man was still there, only now he was on his roof as the water surged around him.

The police came by in a boat and said, "Come on! We'll take you out!"

Again he said, "God will provide."

An hour later, the waters reached to the top of his roof, and he was clinging to his chimney when a police helicopter flew over and dropped a rescue line. "Grab on," they said.

The man shook his head and said, "God will provide." A few minutes later, he slipped under the water and drowned.

When he got to heaven, he confronted God. "How could You let me die like that?"

God shook His head and said, "What did you want? I sent you a police cruiser, a boat, and a helicopter!"

Some people aren't satisfied unless the answers to their prayers *look* supernatural, which is a pride issue. Personally, I'll take my prayers answered in any way, because it's all God. If Crenshaw Christian Center needs new property for some reason, if I have to buy it with tithes and offerings from the church body, I'll do it that way. But if God wants some billionaire to decide to give the church that land, I'll take it that way. Do the things you need to do in the natural to ensure that there are no roadblocks to God meeting your need through natural means, because anytime He wants to He can meet your needs supernaturally and miraculously.

You must constantly apply the yardstick of Scripture—all of Scripture, not just the verses you take out of context. For example, Paul says in Philippians 4:13, "I can do all things through Christ who strengthens me." If you are five feet two inches tall and can't jump over a box, does that mean you will be able to walk out and confess, "I can do all things through Christ who strengthens me," and dunk a basketball? Absolutely not. The promise does not mean that anyone can sing beautifully, automatically be a great cook, or do exceptional athletic feats. What that verse means is that if God has called you to do something, He will strengthen you to do it.

Consider the five-foot-two-inch nonjumper, for example. I believe that if God called that person to preach the gospel in

China, and he or she was chased by the police down an alley that had a large fence at the end, God would enable that person to hurdle that fence at that moment. The next day, however, that same person would be back to having no "hops" as they say in the National Basketball Association.

We must know the whole Bible. If we do, we know that God told the Israelites to cross the Jordan River, but it did not dry up until they put their feet in the water. *How* God meets your need is really none of your business—all you need to do is believe that He has met your need.

## DEVELOP THE HABIT OF MUMBLING

How, exactly, do you come to believe? How do you have faith? God told Joshua, "This Book of the Law shall not depart from your mouth, but you shall meditate in it day and night." The Hebrew word *meditate* means, literally, to "mutter or mumble." It conveys the notion that we should walk around talking to ourselves, saying to ourselves those things that build up our faith. "Thank You, Lord, for a healthy body from the top of my head to the tip of my toes." "Thank You for this day, Father, for the deliverance from debt that You have brought to me." Whatever the issue is, whatever your petition was, go around muttering or mumbling what the Word of God says about it. When you mumble or mutter, at least *you* hear it, and Romans 10:17 says, "Faith comes by hearing, and hearing by the word of God." Look carefully at that verse, though: it does not say, "Faith comes by *having heard*," but by "*hearing*." To understand the full impact of that verse, read it like

121

this: "Faith comes by hearing, and hearing, and hearing, and hearing the Word of God." It doesn't say who you have to hear this from. Hearing it from your own lips is as good as hearing it from anyone else's. In fact, I know my Word is good, so if I hear it from myself, I know that it is accurate and truthful.

Ultimately, the purpose of *meditating* is so that you will "observe" and "do." Merely meditating gets you nowhere, and merely meditating and observing do nothing for you if you do not "do." James 1:22 and 25 say that the person who will be blessed in his deeds is the person who is a "doer" of the Word and not a hearer only. Joshua 1:8 tells us the results of being a "doer" of the Word: "Meditate in it [the Book of the Law] day and night, that you may observe to do according to all that is written in it. For then you will make your way prosperous, and then you will have good success." Joshua did not say *God* would make your way prosperous if you meditated in the law and observed the law and did the law—he said *you* would make your way prosperous. God even added to that by saying, "...and then you will have good success." God was indicating a triple blessing: first that your way would be "prosperous"; then that you would have "success"; and then He amplified that by saying it would be "good" success.

There is another way to look at that. Out here in Los Angeles we have an entertainment industry full of people who are *successful*, with one hit movie or television show after another—yet some of them are never happy. They go through spouse after spouse, some getting divorces and annulments after only a few days. Some have blown fortunes that would stagger ordinary people. Many end up in drug or alcohol rehabilitation, some of them over and over again. Have they had "success"?

---

## God wants His Word to become the essence of your everyday life.

---

Maybe, but it isn't "good success." God said that if you meditate on His Word and observe and do His commandments, you will be prosperous and have "good success." Proverbs 10:22 says, "The blessing of the LORD makes one rich, and He adds no sorrow with it." That tells me the Lord isn't "halfway good"—He is all good, and His gifts are 100 percent good. So, if something comes to you with sorrow, according to this verse, it isn't a blessing. If God gives you money, it will not come with a curse.

This meditation that we have been discussing is for two purposes.

1. To build up your faith to bring your prayer request into physical manifestation sooner rather than later, because "faith comes by hearing"

2. To deflect the devil

Remember through this whole process that you have an enemy. He will try to get you off your confession any way he can, and therefore it is important for you to stay on the offense. Through your constant confession, you are saying to Satan, "I believe I have received this even though you want me to think otherwise. I know what God's promises are concerning [whatever your request is], and I'm standing on those promises." Do you want to know a secret? You cannot think one thing and say another. Whatever you are saying is what you are thinking about, and vice versa. So if God's promises are coming out of your mouth, it's a sure bet that you are also thinking the right thoughts.

Beyond all that, God wants His Word to become the essence of your everyday life. Do you remember how, as a teenager, you would hear songs at the pool or seaside in summer or while driving in your car? These songs—we used to call them the "Top 40"—would play over and over and over again. Sometimes you'd think you'd go crazy if you heard a particular song one more time. But you knew the words, didn't you? I have a friend today who grew up on the Beatles, and today a song can come on by the Beatles, and he still knows every lyric to every song, even if he hasn't heard it in years. Those lyrics became a part of him.

God wants that level of saturation of your soul, to the point that His Word is second nature to you. You won't even have to ask, "Gee, I wonder, *What would Jesus do?*"—the popular phrase from a few years ago. You will know instantly, because you have put the law—that is, God's Word—in your heart.

In fact, when you actually have the Bible in your hands and are studying it, the devil's weapons are pretty limited. He has the spirit of sleep, and often you will find that you get sleepy when you start to study the Word. He also has the spirit of distraction. Have you ever noticed that when you start to study, thoughts pop into your head: *Did I turn off the water? I forgot to put eggs on my grocery list for later today. I hope the kids got where they are going OK.* The phone rings. Someone delivers a package to your door.

These are good reasons for setting aside a time very early in the day to study. It's not impossible for the devil, but in the morning he is more limited in using things like phone calls or deliverymen to interrupt your study time. But he also has the spirit of discomfort. He will make you itch in places you didn't know you had places! You'll notice a pain that you never noticed all week. You'll be hungry. You'll have to go to the bathroom. Anything to keep you from studying the Word!

When Jesus was attacked by the devil, He immediately quoted what was written. Look at Matthew 4:1–11, where the devil tempted Jesus. His first trick to throw Jesus off was doubt.

> Now when the tempter came to Him, he said, "If You are the Son of God, command that these stones become bread."
>
> —MATTHEW 4:3

There are some ministers who say that this indicates that the devil did not know himself if Jesus was the Son of God and was looking for proof. I don't think that's the case. I believe Satan clearly knew, by then, who Jesus was and was trying to get Him to sin. So the first thing he did was to try to plant the seed of doubt in Jesus's mind by saying, "If you are the Son of God…"

You have to admit, it would take a supremely confident and self-assured person who knew who He was to say, "Yep, I am the Son of God, and I don't need to prove it to you!" The human part of Jesus must have been working overtime there, thinking, *Wait a minute; do You think there is a chance I've misled My own self?* How did Jesus win that battle? He quoted the Word:

> But He answered and said, "It is written, 'Man shall not live by bread alone, but by every word that proceeds out of the mouth of God.'"
>
> —MATTHEW 4:4

Each time the devil tempted Him, Jesus responded with, "It is written…"

Obviously, to know what *is written*, you have to read and study it. Jesus knew what was written. More importantly, He knew that it carried the same weight as the spoken word from God Himself. Some of you work in a business where you have a supervisor, and he or she may send around an interoffice memo about some procedure you are to use. That memo carries the same weight as if he spoke to you personally. The Bible is God's "memo" to us.

> Satan may not be the brightest guy
> in the universe, but he is smart
> enough to wait until your study
> time is over to attack you, so it is
> imperative that you know the Word.

Notice, however, that Jesus did not just say, "It is written," then leave it at that. He quoted what was written to the devil: "Man shall not live by bread alone, but by every word that proceeds out of the mouth of God." That showed the devil that Jesus knew what was written and wasn't just guessing. Once He did that, it was the end of the rocks and bread discussion. The devil moved on. Jesus had ended the debate with God's Word.

My wife and I often play Scrabble when we travel on an airplane. In the game, you have to make words out of little wooden squares of letters, and there is a premium on coming up with any word you can find that will use your letters. Sometimes you get desperate. I'll put down, say, *oomrah*.

"That's not a word," Betty says.

I need to get rid of my letters, so I say, "I think it is a word."

We go to the final authority—the dictionary. "No, no *oomrah* in there," she says, and I have to pick my letters back up. This is why you need to meditate day and night. When the devil comes against you, you won't always have your "dictionary" there. You won't always have a Bible handy, and even if you do, you'd have to know where to find what you need. Jesus sure didn't have any scrolls out there in the desert. He had to know it from the inside.

The devil tempted Him again, taking Him up into the holy city and setting Him on the top of the temple:

> And said to Him, "If You are the Son of God, throw Yourself down, for it is written: 'He shall give His angels charge over you,' and 'In their hands they shall bear you up, lest you dash your foot against a stone.' Jesus said to him, "It is written again, 'You shall not tempt the LORD your God.'"
>
> —MATTHEW 4:6–7

Here, the devil changed his tactics. He quoted Scripture to Jesus, but he didn't know enough to quote all of it or to quote it in context. That's the next thing you have to be prepared for. The devil may know enough Scripture to misquote things to you or to quote sections of Scripture without including a context. It is not by accident that some of the worst fanatics in human history have misused the Bible. Adolf Hitler routinely misquoted the Bible or used Old Testament–sounding phrases such as "purity of the blood" and "blood sacrifice" to justify his murder of the Jews.

Other people have deliberately misquoted Scripture for their own ends, including the philosopher Ralph Waldo Emerson, who cleverly and knowingly distorted Scripture to make it say just the opposite of what it says. Hollywood routinely selectively quotes the Bible to make it appear that God favors homosexuality or adultery or other sin. Satan may not be the brightest guy in the universe, but he is smart enough to wait until your study time is over to attack you, so it is imperative that you know the Word.

In 1 Timothy 6:12, it says, "Fight the good fight of faith." We are in a fight; we have an enemy. If you don't fight, Satan will run you through the ringer. Moreover, this is not a *suggestion* that we fight, but a *command*—one of those commands that we are to meditate on, observe, and *do*! It's not an option. This also tells us, however, that faith is a fight, and it's a good fight, which means it's a fight we can win if we use our faith. No fight you lose is a good fight—the only good fights I've ever been in have been those I won. Part of fighting is being ready with your weapon, in this case, Scripture, which is your "sword."

In Matthew 19:16–22, the rich young ruler came to Jesus and asked what he needed to do to inherit eternal life. Jesus said, "Keep the commandments" (v. 17).

This puzzled the man because he had kept the commandments, so he asked, "Lord, which ones?" Jesus listed some of them. The man said, "All these things I have kept from my youth" (v. 20).

Notice that at that point Jesus did not say, "You liar. You have not!" He knew the man had kept them. Why? Because the man was rich. He had been blessed in accordance with Deuteronomy *because* he had kept the commandments from his youth. We know the end of the story, that Jesus knew his heart and asked him to give up some of his material goods, which caused the man to go "away sorrowful, for he had great possessions" (v. 22). In actuality, the possessions had him, and that's why he couldn't give them up.

If we know from Deuteronomy and the story of Abraham that material prosperity is fair game for prayer, and if we have already seen that healing is promised to us, what else can we pray for? Should you pray for such things as patience, self-control, or to be delivered from temptation? Second Peter 1:5 tells us to "add" to our faith virtue, knowledge, self-control, perseverance (or patience), godliness, brotherly kindness, and love. These things, then, are apparently within *our* power to add and only require that we actually add them. God couldn't tell us to *add* something if it was impossible for us to do so.

I believe that things like patience and self-control are not something you can ask God to fix, but rather things you have to fix through the strength of the Holy Spirit He has already put in you. If God would not deliver Jesus from temptation by Satan, why would He deliver you? In fact, through Jesus's actions you have been delivered already, as I discussed earlier. The ball is now in your court.

John even tells us this:

> I write to you, young men, because you have overcome the wicked one.
>
> —1 John 2:13

"Have overcome" is past tense. John was saying they had already "overcome" the wicked one, so if they did it in the past, we must be able to do it now. Therefore, it is already within us, through the Holy Spirit, to overcome the evil one.

In 1 John 1:4, John said that he wrote to the Christians "that your joy may be full." Let's be honest: isn't it easier to be "joy-full" if your stomach is not growling, and if you have a warm place to sleep, and if your needs are met? Yes, it is. John says that it is perfectly fine for us to pray to have our joy be "full." Later on in 3 John 2, John himself says:

> Beloved, I pray [desire, wish] that you may prosper in
> all things and be in health, just as your soul prospers.

I submit to you that John used the term "soul" when he meant "spirit," but it was common for people coming from the Jewish tradition to do that. This is an astounding verse, however, because first it shows that John is praying for the physical, material *prosperity* of others, as well as for their health. So if it is OK for the apostle John to pray for health, material prosperity (even for others), and that Christians prosper "in all *things*," then it must be OK for us to pray for those material blessings and things. What stands out to me in this verse is the way John goes out of his way to separate physical and material blessings from your "soul" prospering. So it is impossible to mess this up and say, "Well, Dr. Price, John just wanted their spirits to be blessed." No! He already said their spirits *were blessed*, but then he went further and said he wanted them blessed in the natural world as well. If it's good enough for John, shouldn't it be good enough for us?

# LET'S REVIEW

Step one in the formula for answered prayer is: *Identify what it is you want God to give you, and then find scriptures that promise that to you.* And if you can't find it in the Bible, it is not promised to you, so don't bother asking.

Now we are ready to move on to the second step in the formula for answered prayer.

# Reflections From "What to Pray For"

_____

_____

_____

_____

_____

_____

_____

_____

_____

_____

_____

_____

_____

# Reflections From "What to Pray For"

_____

_____

_____

_____

_____

_____

_____

_____

_____

_____

_____

_____

# CHAPTER FIVE

# THE PRAYER OF FAITH

*Is anyone among you sick? Let him call for the*
*elders of the church, and let them pray over*
*him, anointing him with oil in the name of*
*the Lord. And the prayer of faith will save the*
*sick, and the Lord will raise him up. And if*
*he has committed sins, he will be forgiven.*
—James 5:14–15

## STEP 2: BELIEVE THAT YOU HAVE WHAT YOU ASK FOR

Once you have identified what you want, and once you have found scriptures that promise that to you, you are ready for step two in the formula for answered prayer: ask God for the things you want, then believe that you have them. Put another way: *ask God for your prayer request in faith.* Note that this begins with "asking." In Matthew 7:7, Jesus said: "Ask, and it will be given to you; seek, and you will find."

Based on what I explained in the last chapter, this asking must be in line with the Bible. It also means that you must pray within the guidelines God has given us, which is to pray to the Father in Jesus's name. Finally, it also means that you must pray in faith. You might wonder, How can I be sure that I am praying in faith? We continually need to be building our faith so that our faith level is equal to the level of the problem that we need solved.

So, what exactly is the prayer of faith? In James 5:14–15, James writes:

> Is anyone among you sick? Let him call for the elders of the church, and let them pray over him, anointing him with oil in the name of the Lord. And the prayer of faith will save the sick, and the Lord will raise him up. And if he has committed sins, he will be forgiven.

Even though James uses healing as his example, the subject I want to deal with is not healing but prayer. Notice that James said, "And the prayer of faith will save the sick." Why didn't he just say, "And prayer will save the sick"?

Do you see my point? The prayer of faith is not the only kind of prayer. There has to be another kind of prayer for James to refer specifically to the "prayer of faith." I've already shown you that there are six distinct types of prayers, but based on one of the verses that we looked at in the last chapter—Mark 11:24—it is clear that James is referring to a petition prayer when he says, "The prayer of faith will save the sick."

By a quick elimination we can prove these things:

- This is not a *prayer of consecration and dedication*, because you aren't *asking* for God's will. You would rightly be acting on the assumption that God's will is that we are healed.

- This is not a *prayer of thanksgiving*, although you would certainly thank God for the healing He has already provided in other circumstances.

- This is definitely not a *prayer of binding and loosing*, unless you could identify a demonic spirit afflicting the person who was ill.

- It might be a *prayer of agreement*, if all the elders and the person who is sick are in agreement.

- It's not really a *prayer of intercession*, because you know what you are interceding for, so you have a specific result to pray for.

- This is a *prayer of faith*, or, as it is also labeled, *petition prayer*. You want God to heal the sick person.

## GOD LIVES ONLY IN THE NOW

Let's get back to the essential requirement for the prayer of faith, as seen in Mark 11:24. The requirement from Jesus is that we have to believe that we receive *when we pray*. Why is that? It turns out that this is a profound and deep revelation about the nature of God. Have you heard the phrases "living for the moment" or "in the now"? Have you ever thought about how impossible that is? As humans, we can never, technically speaking, live in the *now*, because our *nows* instantly become our past—our yesterdays. Put another way, we are temporal creatures. We live within the context of time. For some of you, that's no great revelation. But have you ever really thought about what it means that God does not live in the context or within the confines of time? We pay lip service to the fact that "God is eternal" without really understanding the implications of that.

God doesn't have a tomorrow, and He doesn't have a yesterday. He *won't be* and He *wasn't*. When Moses asked, "Who shall I say sent me?" God said to tell the people, "I AM WHO I AM" (Exod. 3:13–14). He lives in one great big, never-changing,

present tense. Jesus picked up on this too, even in His mortal body. At every opportunity, especially at His trial when the high priests questioned Him, He used the term, "I am." Not only did He know that was a statement of truth, but that statement also drove the Pharisees and religious leaders crazy! "Are You the Christ, the Son of the Blessed?" the high priest asked, and Jesus said, "I am" (Mark 14:61–62).

---

You and I have a *next week*. God
does not. He has only now, and
He is the same every day.

---

For finite creatures such as ourselves, this concept is impossible to truly grasp. Scientists tell us the largest number our mind can comprehend is about one hundred thousand, so even this example won't do justice. But we can at least make a start. Imagine a pelican——you know those ugly birds with the pouch under their beaks to hold fish?——as it swoops down on a beach in California. Rather than picking up a fish, it picks up a single grain of sand. Imagine that somehow that pelican could fly through space and fly all the way to the sun, which is ninety-three million miles from the earth. If somehow that pelican could fly at six hundred miles per hour, it would take that bird eighteen years to cover that distance. Now, imagine that once it gets to the sun, it drops that grain of sand and returns to the earth (eighteen more years), where it picks up another grain of sand. The bird then repeats the process, grain after grain, until it has emptied all the beaches in the world. How long would that take? It's beyond our understanding——but even that would only be the beginning of eternity.

You and I have a *next week*. God does not. He has only now, and He is the same every day. Let me give you a slightly different perspective on this. You have seen a solid gold, smooth wedding ring, correct? Imagine a perfect ring, no noticeable beginning or end, just one continuous ring. Now imagine it spinning, constantly, never starting, never stopping. Think of that as God.

You have heard of lasers, right? They use these stimulated light beams for surgery, target sighting, and all sorts of things. A laser beam typically lasts a tiny fraction of a second——a microsecond. Imagine you are that laser beam—that tiny red dot that is directed at that perfect, eternally spinning ring, and you last all of a tiny fraction of a second, yet that ring is in the air, spinning perfectly every day, no beginning, no end. That's how our physical lives are compared to the eternal presence of God.

It was the same with Jesus when He was in heaven. So it's natural that when Jesus came to earth, He started talking like God, saying, "I am...," always in the present tense. In John's revelation of heaven, the Lord said this:

> I am the Alpha and the Omega, the Beginning and the End...who is and who was and who is to come, the Almighty.... I am alive forevermore.
> —REVELATION 1:8, 18

God's rules have a purpose. He is not a whimsical old man with a long beard and nothing to do all day. Everything He does is timely and orderly. Just consider the universe. The earth and eight other planets revolve around the sun, year after year, in the same place, all spinning and moving with precision. God's orders have a purpose. The reason we must believe when we pray is that God can only hear you in the *now*.

You begin with your words: "Father, I need healing for this diabetes," or "Lord, I need some money to make my car payment."

## YOUR FAITH IS YOUR EVIDENCE

Next, your actions must be consistent with those words. Exactly what do you do? Well, if you prayed for God to provide you with a new car, you do not know how it will come to you. But you had faith when you prayed that God would supply your car. Now, how do you act? One thing you might do is to clean your junk out of your garage. If you believe you will have a car to put in there, you will need some room. If you prayed for new clothes, you can clean out your closet in anticipation of those new clothes arriving. That's what you do when you're *expecting* a baby, right? You decorate the baby's room, buy the baby clothes, and get a crib or playpen. A prayer request is just like that baby, in that you must believe it is as real as that child growing inside a woman, yet which you cannot see (without a sonogram).

In the natural we understand the process of carrying a child for nine months, so we have an easier time expecting a child than we do a prayer request, which could come at any time—but sometimes later rather than sooner. However, the principle is the same: you begin preparing for that request to be answered in the same way you prepare to bring that baby home from the hospital.

We see this principle in Hebrews 11:1:

> Now faith is the substance of things hoped for, the evidence of things not seen.

Faith is *evidence* of things not seen. Faith is evidence. Did you get it? Faith isn't the *thing itself*; it is the evidence of that thing. Think about this: when we go to a trial in a court, the lawyers will introduce evidence. Why do they need evidence for the crime? They need evidence because the jurors were not there at the crime scene to witness what happened. Put another way, they don't have the *thing* itself—the crime.

---

Faith has a certain real, tangible quality.
You may not taste it, see it, or touch
it, but it has substance in heaven.

---

If you go to an airport, you must show a driver's license— evidence of who you are. Why? Because the people checking those IDs were not there when you were born. So they accept the evidence of your birth and see that it matches up to the person in front of them. If you watched me on TV and I asked, "Do I have a body?" you would say yes. But if I asked, "Do I have a brain?" well, I'm sure some of you would say, "That's up for debate!" But most would say yes. Yet how do you know? You can't see it. But you have evidence of it in the fact that I can string two sentences together and make some sense.

When it comes to prayer, your faith itself *is your evidence*, and Paul says in Hebrews that faith has "substance." That is to say, faith has a certain real, tangible quality. Perhaps you cannot taste it, see it, or touch it, but Paul says it has "substance."

Where do you think it has substance? In heaven! Heaven has substance. It may not be the same molecular structure that we have in this physical world, but there are abundant scriptures to indicate that there is substance to heaven.

In John 20:24–25, John wrote:

> Now Thomas, called the Twin, one of the twelve, was not with them when Jesus came. The other disciples therefore said to him, "We have seen the Lord." So he said to them, "Unless I see in His hands the print of the nails, and put my finger into the print of the nails, and put my hand into His side, I will not believe."

Believing is an act of will. Thomas said, "I will not believe." This passage continues with these words:

> And after eight days His disciples were again inside, and Thomas with them. Jesus came, the doors being shut, and stood in the midst, and said, "Peace to you!" Then He said to Thomas, "Reach your finger here, and look at My hands, and reach your hand here, and put it into My side. Do not be unbelieving [or, the traditional King James says, "faithless"] but believing." ...Jesus said to him, "Thomas, because you have seen Me, you have believed. Blessed are those who have not seen and yet have believed."
>
> —JOHN 20:26–27, 29

Jesus apparently had a resurrected physical body that looked very different, because many people did not recognize Him at first after the Resurrection. When the apostle John was on the isle of Patmos, he wrote the Book of Revelation, in which he said he saw God but couldn't really describe Him. John said he saw God sitting on a throne, so there must be some substance to God for Him to sit on a throne.

I don't think God put anything in the Bible by happenstance. I believe that every word is in there for a reason. It's interesting to me that Hebrews 11:1 says, "Now faith is...the evidence of *things not seen.*" What is Paul saying? I believe he is saying that heaven has a substance, that it has things, but not things visible to the human eye or detected by our five physical senses. Heaven's substance—and all the things in it—is detectable by some sense, just not one that we employ here on earth. It is detected through a spiritual sense, but that doesn't mean that this spiritual sense is not every bit as real and as necessary as our physical senses. Friends, when we finally "see" these things with our spiritual senses, we will all be stunned. We'll say, "I was walking right among those angels all this time? I nearly stepped on them."

In 2 Kings 6:8–17, the king of Syria sent an army to destroy Elisha, surrounding Dothan where he resided. Elisha's servant looked at the physical army arrayed against their city and panicked, saying, "Alas, my master! What shall we do?" (v. 15).

Elisha responded, "Do not fear, for those who are with us are more than those who are with them" (v. 16).

This poor servant was looking around at the city walls and didn't see any soldiers, any catapults, or any archers. You can imagine that about that time he was wondering where Elisha

144

got that whiskey. Elisha knew that his servant didn't *see* the same things he saw.

> And Elisha prayed, and said, "LORD, I pray, open his eyes that he may see." Then the LORD opened the eyes of the young man, and he saw. And behold, the mountain was full of horses and chariots of fire all around Elisha.
>
> —2 KINGS 6:17

That angelic army had been there all the time, but Elisha's servant just did not see it.

## SPIRITUAL SUBSTANCE PRECEDES PHYSICAL SUBSTANCE

Everything that exists in our physical, three-dimensional world existed previously in the spirit world. There was a time when nothing existed except God, until He said, "Let there be..." God's world, the spirit world, is a real world. Our physical senses operate in relation to other realities. For example, you can rap your knuckles on a table, and it will hurt! If, however, you put that same wood that your knuckles encountered under an electron microscope, you will find that there are all sorts of spaces between the molecules that constitute that wood. It is matter, but it has spaces between the particles—so many that if you could extract all the spaces, you could put what we call the *wood* on the head of a pin. Even though we cannot depend entirely on our senses to perceive spiritual things, we have to have some type of methodology to discern the spirit world, and that methodology is faith.

Look at Ephesians 1:3: "Blessed be the God and Father of our Lord Jesus Christ, who has blessed us with every spiritual blessing in the heavenly places in Christ." Again, the use of past tense—"has blessed us"—indicates that this is completed—a *done deal,* in our slang. It says Jesus *has already blessed us*—not *will bless us*—and that He has blessed us in "heavenly places." By applying all the teaching in the Bible, we can understand that this only refers to Christians. These blessings are only for those who call Jesus Savior and Master and are not available to anyone else, no matter how sincere they are.

---

Once you get hold of the concept
that the spirit world coexists with this
physical world, and actually preexisted
before this world, then it will no longer
be a mystery how prayers are answered.

---

If you go to a bank, I don't care how sincere you are or what a *good person* you are; if you don't have your name on that account, you will not get money out of that bank. I think it is helpful always to put these things in personal terms, so when I see a verse like Ephesians 1:3, I like to quote it as if God wrote it to me personally. So I meditate on this as though it were written, "Blessed be the God and Father of our Lord Jesus Christ, who has blessed Fred Price with every spiritual blessing in the heavenly places in Christ." Put your name in there!

It takes doing that to really drive home the fact that these are promises *to each of us.*

Technically, it's not even correct to say to a Christian brother or sister, "God bless you," because, according to this, *He already has!* It is awkward not to say that, but it might be better to say, "Enjoy the Lord's blessings!" This is a little thing, but Jesus said that the little foxes spoiled the vines. (See Song of Solomon 2:15.)

If we have been blessed already with "every spiritual blessing in the heavenly places" (Eph. 1:3), what good does that do you if you have a leaky roof or a car that's not running well? We need to remind ourselves that everything exists in spirit form before it ever appears in physical form. The spiritual always precedes the physical. Notice that Ephesians says "every spiritual blessing." The traditional King James Version says "all spiritual blessings." What is left out of "every" or "all"? Nothing, right? Everything that you can imagine being blessed with has already been established by God "in heavenly places."

---

> The blessings of God already exist; the
> things already exist, and it is through
> your faith that you "bring them forth."

---

When speaking to the woman at the well, Jesus said, "God is spirit" (John 4:24). The King James says, "God is *a* spirit." That differentiates God from other spirits, such as angels or demonic spirits. So we are talking about a *spirit God*. And just in case you question how we know that, remember John 1:1 says that Jesus was there with God in the beginning. He ought to know what God is like and who He is.

Once you get hold of the concept that the spirit world coexists with this physical world, and actually preexisted before this world, then it will no longer be a mystery how prayers are answered. John said:

> Immediately I was in the Spirit; and behold, a throne set in heaven, and One sat on the throne. And He who sat there was like a jasper...
>
> —REVELATION 4:2–3

Seats are only designed for those who have a physical form to sit in them. In Revelation 5:1, John says, "And I saw in the right hand of Him who sat on the throne a scroll." From these verses, it's pretty clear that God has a body. He sits on a throne, and He has a right hand (indicating He must also have a left hand). The point is that we know God is a spirit, yet by John's description He also has a physicality. I do not pretend to understand it—it's one of those mysteries. Is it, however, that much different from the fact that our *solid* desk is really full of gaping holes and empty spaces between the molecules? We can't see them, so we say it is *solid*. In truth, it's a little of both—on one level it is *solid*, and on another level it is *as holey as Swiss cheese*. It all depends on which level you are operating.

In Genesis 1:11, God said, "Let the earth bring forth grass, the herb that yields seed, and the fruit tree that yields fruit according to its kind." What is important here is the phrasing, "Let the earth bring forth..." You can only "bring forth" something that has already been there. It didn't say God planted the grass. Now, how this occurred is another teaching, but the point is, it's a similar process to the one discussed in Ephesians where Paul says God has "blessed us with every spiritual blessing in heavenly places."

According to the teaching of Paul in Ephesians 1:3, the blessings of God already exist; the things already exist, and it is through your faith that you "bring them forth." Jesus applied this principle in Matthew 9:29 when He said, "According to your faith, let it be to you." In fact, we have no record, ever, of Jesus crediting His power with a healing or miracle—even though it *was* His power. Instead, He always related the issue to the person's faith.

Hebrews 11:1 begins with an interesting double meaning: "Now faith is..." It's pretty certain that Paul used "now" as a transition phrase from the previous verse, Hebrews 10:39, which says, "But we are not of those who draw back to perdition, but of those who believe to the saving of the soul." Remember, chapter and verse numbers were added by the translators; they were not in the original Greek and are not divinely inspired. They were just put there for our convenience. Look at the double meaning of verse 1: "Now faith is the substance of things hoped for, the evidence of things not seen." It is interesting that this discussion of faith begins with the word *now*. What kind of faith must you have to use the prayer of faith? "Now" faith. Faith deals only with the present, and the "now" kind of faith is the only kind of faith that will work.

## FAITH VERSUS HOPE

Faith is often paired with hope, and it's important to understand the relationship of the two. Hope is the goal setter. But hope has no ability to achieve that goal. If all you have is hope, you are dead. Hope will affect your attitude about the circumstances, but by itself hope cannot *change* the circumstances.

Faith, however, is what achieves the goal and what changes the circumstances. When we discuss the prayer of faith, there is another issue that must be considered. Jesus said, "Whatever things you ask when you pray, believe that you receive them, and you will have them" (Mark 11:24). That statement is based on other biblical principles that we must be aware of. When Jesus said in Matthew 9:29, "... according to your faith let it be to you," He implied that a person's faith could influence one's request. We have returned, then, to the requirement that you have faith sufficient for that which you have asked. Let me make this distinction, though: God has answered your prayer, no matter what level of faith you have. The issue, as far as you are concerned, is that as a finite creature, you only have a certain amount of time. You can't wait forever. So, to use a monetary example, if you have a faith request in prayer of something equivalent to $1 million, but you only have $1 faith, you might be dead by the time you've exercised enough faith to bring that into manifestation.

I suggest people begin by practicing
their faith on things that are not
going to kill them or bankrupt
them if they don't attain it, if their
faith comes up a little short.

It's not God as such who brings things and dumps them into your lap. It is God who has provided those things, and it is God, through His Son, who has given you the authority to obtain those things, but it's your faith that pulls those things from the faith realm into the physical realm. If your faith is focused on something so big that you cannot pull it to where you can visually see it, it won't come to pass. This concept is difficult and is one of the keys to why people don't see more answered prayer—usually they have not understood that their faith plays a role in the prayer. They are expecting God to do it all. The catch is, God has *already* "done it all," and now you have to do your part.

A great example of this is our electric power generating system. Those giant dynamos provide all the power we need. That power courses through the electric grid and through lines to our homes; eventually that power is wired into our lights. But you do not get any light—no matter how many kilowatts are being pushed out of that system—until you *turn on the switch*. "Yeah, but doesn't the power company know I need some light and heat?" Of course they do, and they have provided it, but you will sit there in the cold and dark until you turn on that switch. Crying about it won't change things. Begging the power company won't change things. The power company has already done its part! Now you must do yours.

I realize that, for some people, this is a tough teaching. "You mean, Pastor Price, that I haven't gotten my healing because I don't have enough faith?" That's a possibility. This is not "blame the victim," but we cannot hide behind politically correct-sounding phrases that impede us from using the Word of God as God wants us to employ it.

Instead, let's reorient ourselves as to how we look at heaven. Everything that has ever been, or ever will be, already exists in heaven. God has already made it. There is no shortage of any of these things. Do you really think that when someone prays for an MP3 player, God actually says, "Hmmm. Wish I had thought of that! OK, I'll create one right now"? No! Solomon told us there is nothing new under the sun (Eccles. 1:9). If you read the Old Testament prophecies, you will see references to things that seem weird, such as chariots with smoke coming out or whirlwinds that attack people, and yet if you understand that prophecy is layered, some of those things clearly are references to modern technology—cars, tanks, airplanes—and perhaps other things that haven't even been invented yet on earth. But God sees the end of human time, and believe me, He's seen it all.

Tithing is an area where you can check
your level of faith. Can you believe
God enough to give Him 10 percent
and have faith that He will meet your
needs with the other 90 percent?

When people come to me saying they haven't gotten their prayers answered, I have to ask them what their faith level is. You might think, *Oh, no! I may never have enough faith.* Quite the contrary, I think if you approach this methodologically, you can have a pretty good idea of your faith level at any given time on any given thing. Ask, "What can I believe God for?" I mean, what can you *really* believe God for? I suggest people begin by practicing their faith on things that are not going to kill them or bankrupt them if they don't attain it, if their faith comes up a little short.

For example, let's take healing. You can't wait until you have cancer, then suddenly say, "I believe I'm healed." There might exist that rare person who can immediately boost his or her faith to that level, but these people are one in a million, like the people who can write wonderful songs or conceive of brilliant mathematical ideas. We are talking here about average people—not the faith phenoms. So you cannot wait until you have a life-threatening disease to suddenly decide you're going to *believe* in faith healing. Instead, build your faith for healing by using your faith on minor medical maladies, like headaches or maybe a small infection.

My wife has an excellent book, titled *Through the Fire and Through the Water*, about her attack of cancer several years ago. She prayed over her health every day, but neither she nor I knew that you also had to do the right things in the natural when it comes to your body. You can't eat sixty Snickers bars a day and pray, "Lord, keep me thin!" We understood later that she had a terrible diet and had not practiced good, healthful eating her entire life. So when the cancer hit—and it was a big tumor—she and I fought it in faith for quite some time. But finally we got some revelation on this. That tumor had a head start of many, many years inside her body. It was growing long before she even knew about it, and it grew more after we began to fight it in faith.

We learned that it is absolutely fine to use modern medical science when you need to. In cases of a heart attack or something like that, you may be unconscious, so you can't use your faith. Or you may get an attack like my wife's tumor with such a head start that by the time we caught up to it in faith, she would be dead. (I've used the example of Carl Lewis, one of the fastest runners on the earth at one time. Even if you have Carl Lewis racing me, if you spot me two feet from the ribbon, I'm going to win that race. No matter how fast he is, my head start is too great!)

When we got my wife medical help in the natural, then that faith was magnified and given a chance to work. I won't go into great detail, but the doctors were absolutely astounded that she recovered so quickly. They had never seen anything like that. That was her faith.

Well, in that same vein, you must use your faith on things that are not going to kill you. Destroy the little dragons first before you take on that big fire-breather. That will have a two-fold effect. First, obviously, it will answer your immediate request. Second, it will build your confidence in your faith, just as it builds your faith itself. Now you can tackle something a little bigger. Maybe you used your faith, as we did, on a car payment. Once you can believe God for that car payment, next you can believe God for a whole car.

I went through this process when we first started in faith. Betty and I made a decision to tithe. Based on Malachi 3:8–10, we decided we had to tithe if we ever wanted to get out of our financial bondage.

Look at those verses, where God says:

> "Will a man rob God?
> Yet you have robbed Me!
> But you say,
> 'In what way have we robbed You?'
> In tithes and offerings.
> You are cursed with a curse,
> For you have robbed Me,
> Even this whole nation.
> Bring all the tithes into the storehouse,
> That there may be food in My house,
> And try Me now in this,"
> Says the LORD of hosts,
> "If I will not open for you the windows of heaven

155

> And pour out for you such blessing
> That there will not be room enough to receive it."
> —MALACHI 3:8–10

I had not understood that the reason He wanted my 10 percent was not because He needed the money, but because He wanted to free me. But I was bull-headed: "I ain't gonna give no preacher none of my money," I said. Then I learned that I wasn't giving my money to a preacher; I was giving it to God. Of course you have to use wisdom to make certain that the church that you give to or the ministry you tithe to is benefiting the people. You need to sow your good seed into good ground.

Tithing is an area where you can check your level of faith. Can you believe God enough to give Him 10 percent and have faith that He will meet your needs with the other 90 percent? I have found that not only will He meet your needs, but He will also exceed your expectations with that 90 percent. This is not to boast, but just to inform: Betty and I tithe 40 percent, and we have more money than we ever dreamed. I pay bills, in full, the minute they come in. Here's the point, though: We didn't start that way. We started believing for those bills to be paid.

## FACTORS THAT CAN IMPEDE YOUR PRAYER OF FAITH

There are some other components to working the prayer of faith. I have talked about your degree of faith. As Jesus said, you only need faith the size of a mustard seed to do incredible things. (See Matthew 17:20.) However, there are some other things, some "mitigating factors," as they would say in a court-room, that can impede even the most impressive faith.

For example, you cannot be engaged, on a regular, conscious basis, in sin and expect God to reward your faith. If you aren't married, you and your *significant other* cannot be shacked up and think that you will get answers to your *prayer of agreement.* It won't work. You can't be a practicing homosexual and think God will look the other way, or a businessman or woman who cheats employees or customers and thinks God will prosper your business. That won't happen. Sinful living short-circuits the whole system. It's not enough just to do the right things in the right order. You must also make sure that you are living right. Of course I'm not talking about a slip-up, where someone messes up one time and genuinely repents, but even that can have an effect.

---

> ## "Is there something in your life that might be interfering with or short-circuiting your prayer request?"

---

Let's say you were believing for a new job, and, for you, this was a large *order,* faith-wise. But you have been diligently working on it, believing sincerely, and praying the right way. But it's been some time, and you still don't have your new job. You may not be aware of it, but in the spirit world, God has been moving things around. You are just about to get a call or a letter for an interview for that new job. But before that can happen, you go out and willfully sin. Even though you had been climbing that faith hill and were close to the top (even though you didn't know it), now you slide back down a couple of hundred yards and have to make up all that ground lost due to sin. The sad thing is that if you had known how close you were, it's likely that you would not have engaged in that behavior. Still, it has an effect. Actions have consequences, both in the spirit world and in the physical world.

When people come to me for counseling about unanswered prayer, I first make sure they are doing the right things in terms of their prayer life. If they are, then I ask them to check out their lives. "Is there something in your life that might be interfering with or short-circuiting your prayer request?" I ask them. Some people call this the "checkup from the neck up."

So far we have discussed two ingredients for answered prayer:

1. Determine what you want, then find scriptures that promise that to you.
2. Ask the Father for what you want in the name of Jesus, and believe you have received it.

Along the way, you must constantly evaluate your level of faith to make sure it is equal to that which you have requested. At the same time, eliminate any *short-circuits* that might arise from wrong living. Be persistent. Stay patient. I know a fellow who loves football. He sometimes watches the Monday night football game. At times he will start watching that game, turn it off after one quarter or at halftime, and say, "That's a blowout. This other team has no chance." Then he will pick up the paper the next morning and find that the team made a fourth-quarter comeback and won the game. You may be denying yourself some great faith victories by quitting in the third quarter.

## SPEAK YOUR PRAYER REQUESTS

Let's be a little more specific about this "asking" process. It is absolutely essential that you speak your prayer requests. A silent prayer will get a silent answer. In Romans 10:8, Paul quotes Deuteronomy and asks about faith:

> But what does it say? "The word is near you, in your mouth and in your heart" (that is, the word of faith which we preach).

For prayer to work, you must *say it*, not think, it. Speaking is how you release your faith. You might say, "But preacher, you just told us that the model prayer for Christians was Mark 11:24, and it doesn't tell us to *say* there." Oh, yes, it does! If you back up to the context of that verse in Mark 11:22–23, you will see Jesus is talking about faith and prayer, and He said, "Have faith in God. For assuredly, I *say* unto you, whoever *says* to this mountain, 'Be removed and be cast into the sea,' and does not doubt in his heart, but believes that those things he *says* will be done, he will have whatever he *says*" (emphasis added). It is abundantly clear from the setting of Mark 11:24 that Jesus meant that prayer needed to be spoken. That is how you release

159

your faith—through your mouth, and we are discussing the prayer of faith here. I must *say*. If I do not say, I did not pray; I merely thought. Jesus didn't say, "Whoever *thinks* about the mountain, that it will be cast into the sea, will have whatever he *thinks*."

---

> If people don't hear, they can't believe, and if they don't believe, they can't receive, which means they can't get saved.

---

The Bible is very specific. When it is dealing with the life of the mind and thought, it uses the word *mind* or *thought*. Philippians 2:5 says, "Let this mind be in you which was also in Christ Jesus." In Isaiah 55:8 God said, "For My thoughts are not your thoughts." If Jesus meant we could just think our prayers, He would have said so.

At first, you might think (or say!), "That's silly. Why do I have to do it like that?" I'm not entirely sure how it works, but we find an inkling of it in the first chapter of the Bible where it continually repeats the phrase, "Then God said..." He didn't just project a thought, and He didn't just visualize the sun, moon, and stars. Why it involves speaking, I don't know, except over and over again we see the emphasis of words in the Bible. We read earlier: "So then faith comes by hearing [words], and hearing by the word of God" (Rom. 10:17).

We may later find out, when we meet the Lord, the actual physics of how this happens. For example, we know that words are energy, and energy itself has measurable substance. Put another way, words themselves are substance, even if you can't see them and even if they consist only of microscopic proportions. Imagine the substance in the spoken words of God Almighty! Now, if we are like Jesus, and He is like the Father, and Jesus has imparted Himself to us, and the Holy Spirit fills us, then would not our words take on greater import? Would they not have even more substance?

Faith to speak comes from what? Romans 10:17 says it comes from hearing, not "having heard," but from hearing…and hearing…and hearing. If you hear something enough, you begin to believe it. We have no problem with this concept in the natural. Child psychologists will tell you that you can destroy a child's self-esteem by saying things like, "You will never amount to anything," or "You are a loser!" We take great care to praise our children for what they do right, because even though they may be doing something wrong, we want to focus them on right behavior. So we say things like, "That was a great pitch, son," or "You look beautiful in that dress." Even if at that moment the boy had made an average pitch, or even if the girl looked plain as a mud fence, you essentially are speaking faith to the circumstances. As *they* hear it, they begin to believe it, and as they believe it, they develop confidence. A poor pitcher with confidence is better than a great pitcher with no confidence. And even people in the makeup and fashion industry will point out certain people who really are not that attractive, yet they just have that aura of confidence that makes other people see them as attractive. That attractiveness is an aura that comes from confidence, which, in part, has come from the fact that a person has heard and believed what was said earlier. When it comes to the gospel, faith comes by hearing, and hearing comes from preaching the Word of God. That's why Jesus commissioned us to go into all the world and preach the gospel to every creature. If people don't hear, they can't believe, and if they don't believe, they can't receive, which means they can't get saved.

Once you have identified the thing you desire, found scriptures that promise you that, and have prayed to the Father in Jesus's name, believing that you have received it at the time you prayed, then you are ready for step three, affirming your confession.

# Reflections From "The Prayer of Faith"

_____

_____

_____

_____

_____

_____

_____

_____

_____

_____

_____

_____

_____

## Reflections From "The Prayer of Faith"

_____

_____

_____

_____

_____

_____

_____

_____

_____

_____

_____

_____

_____

_____

# CHAPTER SIX

# AFFIRMING YOUR
# ANSWERED PRAYER

*This is how you build stronger faith: by
confessing what God's Word says and
hearing with your own ears those words.*

## STEP 3: AFFIRM WHAT YOU HAVE ASKED FOR

Once you have prayed, believing you have received it, you are ready for ingredient number three—let every thought and desire affirm that you have what you have asked God for. Don't doubt your own prayer. Begin to see yourself as having that prayer already fulfilled, even if you do not see it in the natural. You need to thank God daily for answering that prayer. It's important to understand that this is not a confession of the physical fact, because you cannot lie. In the natural you do not see it yet. But 2 Corinthians 5:7 says, "For we walk by faith, not by sight." Another way of putting that is, "For we walk by faith in what God has already provided, not by the senses that tell us otherwise." Remember that the spirit world coexists with this natural world, and something can be completely real in the spirit world, yet we are oblivious to it.

Many people today, deep down in theirs spirits, are aware of this other world, the spirit world. That is the reason movies like *The Exorcist* and television shows like *Ghost Whisperer* or *Medium* do so well. Sometimes it isn't *cool* or *hip* to admit it, but man's interest in ghosts, spirits, and so forth comes from a deep-seated knowledge that it is real. Ghosts are real—they are spirits, and Jesus said God was a spirit, so these spirit creatures act in a world or in another dimension that we cannot see. We have no trouble suspending our sense-based reality when we watch one of those shows, yet when it comes to God, that seems to be another issue.

Here, then, is ingredient three: confess your request as a faith fact. Physical facts are based on sensory or scientific evidence, while faith facts are based on God's Word. What has God said about this thing? By praying daily, "Thank You, Father, I believe my debts are paid," or "Thank You, Lord, I believe I am healed," you are also adding to your faith. In Romans 10:17, Paul says, "So then faith comes by hearing and hearing by the word of God." This is how you build stronger faith—or at least take one step in building stronger faith—by confessing what God's Word says and hearing with your own ears those words.

## The Difference Between Believing and Knowing

It is important to understand the difference between *believing* and *knowing*. Despite what might appear to be clear-cut teaching, you'd be surprised how difficult it is for some people to get this distinction. As an illustration, let me ask if you believe without a shadow of a doubt that you are reading this book. If you do, raise your hand, even though you may be all alone there. Think about that, now: Why would you *believe* you are reading this book? Don't you *know* it? If you can see it, feel it, taste it, touch it, and so on, you do not need any faith. Faith only deals with that which cannot be perceived by the senses.

---

Bringing your every thought into line with your prayer is no easy task. Your enemy, the devil, will try to drag you back into the world of the senses every step of the way, and you must fight him.

---

Notice that in Genesis God doesn't offer any evidence as to His existence. He just began the book, "In the beginning, God..." You have heard, many times in your life, I'm sure, comments such as, "You can never prove the Bible," or "You can't prove Jesus rose from the dead." And that is correct. We have good evidence about all of the historical statements in the

Bible—overwhelming evidence, I believe—the kind of evidence that would stand up in any court showing that Jesus rose from the grave. Yet we do not have evidence that leaves you "without a doubt." God did that on purpose. If He provided evidence beyond a doubt, we would not need faith, and God is a faith God. He demands that we come to Him in faith, not on the basis of evidence that leaves you without a choice.

Theoretically, you might say, "I don't believe in gravity," but you will conduct your life 100 percent in alignment with the theory of gravity as if you did believe it. So that really is not a choice. God will not force you to do anything or to believe anything. He will give you plenty of evidence, but there will always be a little something unproven so that you have to take it on faith.

Another example of how you take things on faith all the time without realizing it is this: Do you have a brain? How do you know? You've never seen it! You accept it as fact because medical science has told us that you need a brain for many functions—including reading this book. It underscores, however, the fact that we do not *know* everything through the five senses, just as the philosopher John Locke claimed in his famous book *An Essay Concerning Human Understanding*. We are not a "blank slate" or a *tabula raza* as he claimed, only learning things through touch, taste, hearing, smelling, and sight. Otherwise, how would you ever learn the word *learn*? Or *love*? You can't taste *democracy* or smell *before* or hear *until*. All these ideas come to your brain—which you can't see—through learning processes that you can't see, taste, hear, smell, or touch.

Bringing your every thought into line with your prayer is no easy task. Your enemy, the devil, will try to drag you back into the world of the senses every step of the way, and you must fight him. James 4:7 is relevant here. Most people quote that verse as, "Resist the devil and he will flee from you." There is more to that verse, however. The full verse says, "Therefore submit to God. Resist the devil and he will flee from you." *Submitting* comes before *resisting*. Some of you resist a great deal, with no effect, because you are not submitted. You must put yourself in God's hands. In the physical world, we do this all the time without a second thought.

You climb into an airplane and head for New York City. Who is flying the plane? Not you! You've placed your life in the hands of some man or woman you don't even know, whom you've never met, and you don't even know if the person has ever graduated from flying school! It's all *assumed* because of human experience. You've done it before, so it must be OK. You go into a hospital and allow some person you've never met to put a mask over your mouth and say, "Count backward from ten." You think the doctors are going to take out your appendix or fix some problem—but have you ever seen their medical degrees? Do you know that there are examples of doctors amputating the wrong leg or leaving sponges or other items in the body after operations? Of course, the vast majority do *not* do that, but I'm just making a point that it seems to be remarkably easy for us to put ourselves in the hands of *men* we don't know rather than God whom we do know!

Peter reiterated the fact that we are in a fight with the devil for the control of our thought life. In 1 Peter 5:8 he wrote, "Be sober, be vigilant; because your adversary the devil walks about like a roaring lion, seeking whom he may devour." This passage is significant because it shows:

1. We have an adversary.
2. He is not a "roaring lion" but would like you to think he is.
3. He cannot "devour" you unless you let him!

If you are "sober" and "vigilant," your adversary cannot do anything to you. We must constantly keep our guard up, but the good news is that he can't do anything without our cooperation. Put another way, he can't do anything without our permission.

Part of that permission is denying him any access to your mind. Bring every thought into line with what you have asked. Let every desire affirm that you have what you have prayed for. In an earlier chapter I described my battle with a tumor when I was a young man. When I had that tumor, every morning the devil would ask me the same question: "How do you feel?" He was determined to get me onto the playing field of the senses, of feelings.

I had to be just as determined not to play on his home field, so every day, even though that tumor was still in my body—and very sore to the touch!—I had to confess, "Get out of here, devil. I believe I'm healed." Again, I was not confessing a lie. I did not "call those things which are as though they were not," but rather I called those things which were not (that I was healed) as though they were.

## The Devil's Weapons

When it comes to the battlefield of the mind, which is where this principle is fought out, two of the devil's biggest weapons are *fear* and *friends*. Without question, the devil's number one knockout punch is fear. If he can get you thinking, *This tumor is malignant. I'm going to die. My prayer won't be answered before I die*, then he has you. Fear and faith cannot coexist.

One way to discipline yourself against fear is to check things out in the natural and show Satan you are not afraid. When you have a pain somewhere, and the devil is saying, "See, that's cancer. You have cancer," it would be an act of fear *not* to go to the doctor and get it checked out.

Instead, you should be saying, "Devil, I rebuke you in the name of Jesus. And to show you that I believe I'm healed, I'm going in today for an X-ray that will prove this isn't cancer." Some people avoid doctors or hospitals or checkups out of a *lack of faith*, because they are afraid of what the doctor might find. Don't be so foolish as to confuse your faith *in healing* with your faith in *not going to a doctor*. In the latter case, you're operating out of fear, not faith.

Our modern one-click world leaves
us somewhat unrealistic in our beliefs
about what real patience is. Some prayer
requests require years of confession.

Every time Jesus came to the disciples supernaturally, the first thing He said was, "Fear not!" Before you can get into faith, you have to get rid of fear, or, put another way, you can get rid of fear by confessing your faith. Again, do not ignore those steps you can take in the natural world to ensure that you aren't leaving some door open. For example, with my tumor, I did go to the doctor and found the tumor was not malignant, so I could eliminate the fear of it killing me. That was an advantage. My wife, Betty, had a more serious challenge when she battled her tumor, because it could have metastasized and spread throughout her body. So her faith was challenged in ways mine was not.

Or if you are in debt and praying for deliverance from debt, keep checking the want ads for jobs if you don't have one. You cannot just sit on your duff believing God will drop money into your lap. Most of the time, that money will come through the hands of man.

Satan also uses friends—some of them sincere, well-meaning Christians—to attack your confession. If your friends don't understand what you are doing or how faith works, they will say things like, "Aunt Doris had that kind of cancer, and she died!" Or, "My cousin Louis lost his job, and they ended up taking away his house!" You absolutely cannot allow even good-hearted friends to deflect your confession of affirmation. Even spouses (and this is where the prayer of agreement is relevant) have to be on the same page with your confession, or they can say things that will torpedo your prayer requests by getting you into negative confessions. "Well, maybe I wasn't meant to have that car." "God just didn't want me moving to Nevada at this time." God didn't have anything to say about your car or your move. Your friends put those ideas into your head. It's very hard, especially for people who really don't understand the so-called "Faith Movement," for people to be supportive in your confession when in the natural they don't see anything. Sometimes, to get what you want, you have to isolate yourself from some of your well-meaning friends and relatives. Jesus frequently went off by Himself. I'm convinced that after a while, even He had to get away from Thomas and the other doubters.

Friends will often come to you under the subterfuge of being *concerned* about your situation. Some of them may be concerned about your situation, but far more are concerned that you are going to achieve success where they have failed, and in essence they are trying to talk you out of success. If they say something to you that is not in line with your prayer confession, just reply, "Well, praise God, I know that I am promised [fill in the promise here], and I still believe I have received it. But thank you for your concern." Then change the subject!

> ## As you master smaller faith issues,
> ## you can begin to believe God
> ## for larger and larger requests.

Peter told us that we had to add patience to our list of virtues. (See 2 Peter 1:5–7.) *We* had to add it—God wasn't going to add it for us. Our modern one-click world leaves us somewhat unrealistic in our beliefs about what real patience is. Some prayer requests require years of confession.

Let me give you an example of how consistent you have to be with your confirmation that affirms your prayer. I know an author in the Midwest who, years ago, began writing a history book. It was a large undertaking, covering all two hundred plus years of American history and then some, and it took more than a decade to research and write. All the time he was writing that book, he told me that he was confessing, "Thank You, Lord, for giving me a publisher for this book." Before he had it halfway written, he was already focusing on receiving a publisher. His book was somewhat controversial, so in the natural it was questionable if he would ever get it published. So he had to focus on his confession that God would provide a publisher.

Sure enough, when it was completed, he had not one, but two offers from publishers, each with a nice advance. As soon as he had a publisher, he began confessing the success of the book in the marketplace, even though it was an eight-hundred-page nonfiction, hardcover book. Still, he began confessing it would be a best seller. This was more than a year before the book actually appeared in print. But he was consistent, and when it finally came out, it received accolades from the *Wall Street Journal* and the *New York Times*, and it was indeed a best seller. He told me that he had essentially been praying and confessing that result for upwards of *ten years*, but it worked.

Not only did that episode result in answered prayer, but it gave him *faith evidence* for his next prayer request. The next time he prays about something of the same nature, it shouldn't take ten years at all, but a fraction of that time to get what he has asked for.

---

> In order for you to have success
> with your prayer requests, you
> may have to move out of range
> of those negative comments.

---

I've used the following example before as well. Many of you have worked out in a gym or fitness center. If you have ever lifted weights, you know that you do not walk over to the weight rack and take the heaviest dumbbells and hoist them over your head. You'll sprain something if you do! Instead, you begin with a weight you can lift, then push yourself to the limit on that weight. Then incrementally you build up the weights, until at some point you will be "pumping iron" like you never thought possible. Faith works by the same process. As you master smaller faith issues, you can begin to believe God for larger and larger requests.

## STEP 4: GUARD AGAINST EVERY EVIL THOUGHT THAT COMES INTO YOUR MIND

Having determined what it is you want, and having found scriptures that promise you that; having asked the Father for it in Jesus's name, and having believed you have received it; and having brought every thought and desire in line to affirm that you have received what you asked for, you are now ready for ingredient four, which is: Thoughts are governed by observation, association, and teaching. Guard against every evil thought that comes into your mind.

Bringing thoughts in line with your confession requires good observation, profitable association, and solid teaching. Good observation involves being able to see things through the eyes of faith and not fear. This is where many people get off track. Looking at things through the eyes of faith is not like the Black Knight in the Monty Python movie who has his arm cut off and says, "It's just a flesh wound." No, that's a lie. But it's every bit as much of a lie to immediately say, "I just know I'm going to get the flu this year." This is especially true if you haven't gotten the flu before. Why in the world—based on your good observation—would you ever say something like that? Seeing things through the eyes of faith requires good (that is, honest, objective) observation so that you don't fall into fear. When my wife, Betty, had cancer, the doctors said,

"We need to treat this with chemotherapy and radiation to kill it." Faith said, "Fight this war on all fronts, spiritual and physical. Take the treatments." She did, and she is fully recovered with no sign of cancer in her for years.

I've already discussed your associations and friendships. Associations that can hinder your faith may also be your church, if it does not reinforce the faith message you are hearing. "God may want you sick for a reason," you may hear, or "God took your business away to make you humble." I have a book titled *Why Should Christians Suffer?* in which I deal with these kinds of comments, but the bottom line is that God does not want you sick or poor. In order for you to have success with your prayer requests, you may have to move out of range of those negative comments. You might even have to change churches.

It can even come down to family situations. I had a note given to me the last time I taught this subject in church. The person asked, "What about family members that you have to stay with? I have a sister who talks opposite of the Word. I do not listen to her. I put the Word first. What should I do?"

That's a good question. To follow my suggestion is obviously (in this situation) going to cause a conflict, especially if you don't have much choice. For instance, a youngster living at home with parents or other relatives is not really capable of living on his or her own. So you will have to deal with this on a case-by-case basis. If you can't leave, put on headphones as you walk around, and listen to faith-filled tapes. In the case of a job, you have to operate in a workplace, and you can't just

177

leave your job. Still, you need to protect yourself somehow. When people insist on making negative comments, maybe you just have to buck the trend. "We'll never get that raise," someone will say.

You might have to say, "Well, praise God, I believe I'm getting my raise this year."

The verse that you want to use as a foundation for bringing every thought and desire in line with your prayer and confession is Philippians 4:8:

> Finally, brethren, whatever things are true, whatever things are noble, whatever things are just, whatever things are pure, whatever things are lovely, whatever things are of good report, if there is any virtue and if there is anything praiseworthy—meditate on these things.

Note that Paul followed the characteristic "true" with "noble," "just," "pure," "lovely," "of good report," and "virtue." Something can be true—Sammy is cheating on his wife, or Susie is lying on her tax return—but they are not noble, lovely, or of good report. This is especially relevant when it comes to listening to gossip. It doesn't matter if something is true— your standard is different. Not only does it have to be true, but it also must be virtuous and of good report. If what someone wants to tell you isn't virtuous, noble, of good report, *and* true, then you have no business listening to it.

In 2 Corinthians 10 these principles are amplified:

> Though we walk in the flesh, we do not war according to the flesh. For the weapons of our warfare are not

carnal [or fleshly] but mighty in God for pulling down strongholds, casting down arguments and every high thing [the traditional King James says "imaginations"] that exalts itself against the knowledge of God, bringing every thought into captivity to the obedience of Christ, and being ready to punish all disobedience when your obedience is fulfilled.

—2 CORINTHIANS 10:3–6

The command to bring every thought into captivity to the obedience of Christ tells me that I must be capable of bringing that into captivity. God would know if that is something I can or cannot do.

---

## Your mind is a mailbox. It is impossible for you to prevent a thought from coming, but what happens next is up to you.

---

We see how important all this is with the use of the term *war*. If Satan can dominate your thinking, he can control your life without ever laying a hand on you. The battlefield is in your mind. When Paul says "casting down arguments and every high thing," it means we are to unload anything that is contradictory to the Word of God. Knowledge of God comes through His Word. The term *imagination* is interesting, because humans can have some wild imaginations. Unless you

179

are sick in the head, you don't sit around thinking or imagining ways to be *worse* off than you currently are. *Gee, I wonder what I'd do if suddenly I lost everything?* No, more often than not people imagine what they would do if they inherited a million dollars. People's imaginations can run wild, so you must submit your thoughts and imaginations to the Word of God. If it doesn't compute, delete it. If it doesn't measure up, cast it down; throw it in the Dumpster. God said we had the power to do that, so we have the power to do it.

When, in defining ingredient four, I say, "Thoughts are governed by observation, association, and teaching," and that you should "guard against every evil thought that comes into your mind," let me clarify something. You have no control over what thoughts will come to you. Indeed, as soon as I say, "Don't think pink!" you immediately think "pink." What you do have control over is what thoughts stay and what you do with those thoughts—especially whether you act on them or not. Your mind is a mailbox. You have no control over what the postal people put in that mailbox, and I'm sure you get your share of what we call *junk mail*. These are usually advertisements for products or services you don't want. What happens to most of that junk mail? It ends up in the garbage, right? I don't even open some of mine. If I can tell it's junk mail, it's sent straight to Mr. Garbage. That's the way thoughts are. It is impossible for you to prevent a thought from coming, but what happens next is up to you.

Jesus said, "Whoever looks at a woman to lust for her has already committed adultery with her in his heart." If you are a normal American man, and some knockout woman comes down the street, your eyes will see her. It is just a fact that unless your head is down and you are reading the stock market quotations, you will see the woman. Is that committing adultery? No. But if you look at her to lust for her—in other words, when that thought comes, *My, she sure is fine!*—you need to change the subject immediately in your mind. Think something like: "...and isn't it a beautiful day."

## STEP 5: THINK CONSTANTLY ON THE PROMISES ON WHICH YOU BASE THE ANSWER TO YOUR PRAYER

Let's move on to ingredient number five: think constantly on the promises on which you base the answer to your prayer. Focus on God's Word, which has promised you that thing for which you prayed. Keep your mind on the promise, not on the request. Proverbs 4:20–22 helps us to understand how to do this:

> My son, give attention to my words;
> Incline your ear to my sayings.
> Do not let them depart from your eyes;
> Keep them in the midst of your heart;
> For they are life to those who find them,
> And health to all their flesh.

These commands show us that we are in control of what we give attention to, what we incline our ears to, and what we keep in our hearts. Words, the writer says, are "life...and health," but only to those who "find them." The Hebrew word for "health" here is literally "medicine," but medicine does you no good if you won't take it.

---

Keep your eyes on God's promises,
for those He will not break.
If He has promised it to you,
then you are entitled to it.

---

Matthew 8:17 says, referring to Jesus, "He Himself took our infirmities and bore [literally, "carried"] our sicknesses." It's obvious to me that if Jesus took them and bore them, then He must not have wanted me to have them. Yet the Word will be healing salve—a medicine to you—only if you know this verse and apply it to your health situation. Look at 1 Peter 2:24: "...who Himself bore our sins in His own body on the tree, that we, having died to sins, might live for righteousness—by whose stripes you were healed." This is almost exactly what Matthew wrote. So if your prayer is for healing, ingredient five says see yourself healed. Focus only on the promise of God that Jesus *carried* (past tense again) your sickness and healed you with His stripes. Make plans as though your disease did not affect you.

Betty had a sister who contracted cancer, and she grew weaker. We tried to minister to her, to get her in an environment where she would hear things in line with the Word. We would say, "Tina, you have to eat. If you don't eat, your body won't be strong, and you won't be able to get up and move about."

She would reply, "Yes, but the doctor said I couldn't." Her faith was in what the doctor told her, not what God told her.

We have seen countless times where doctors say that so-and-so will never walk again. Yet, before you know it, that person was playing college football or active on a tennis team. Doctors are human, and most of them are going by natural medical science, which is based on averages. It says that on average, with such-and-such a condition, you will not walk again. But God's Word is all about the exceptions. Noah was an exception—only Noah and his wife and kids escaped that storm, out of the entire world! Joshua and Caleb were exceptions. Out of all those Israelites who came out of Egypt, only those two entered the Promised Land. You need to know that you will walk, or you will be healthy, or you will get out of debt not because you are the statistical exception—but because you are following God's promises.

Some people expect miracles to bail them out, but you will not find one scripture in the New Covenant that promises you a miracle. If God wants to work one in your life, fine, but that is not a promise. Instead, you must keep your eyes on God's promises, for those He will not break. If He has promised it to you, then you are entitled to it.

In John 15:7 Jesus says, "If you abide in Me, and My words abide in you, you will ask what you desire [the traditional King James says "ask what you will"] and it shall be done for you." Note the condition here is that you abide in Him and His words abide in you. That word *abide* means "to settle down in or take up residence in you." So we could read John 15:7 like this: "If you settle down in and take up residence in Me, and My words settle down in and take up residence in you, you will ask what you desire, and it shall be done for you."

## Step 6: Think on the Love, Mercy, Goodness, and Blessings of God

Ingredient six in the formula for answered prayer is this: in your waking moments, think on the love, mercy, goodness, and blessings of God, and it will boost your faith. God has shown me so much goodness and mercy that at times I think I must be His favorite child, but in reality I know that we are all "favorite children" of the most high God. Earlier in this teaching I referred to Philippians 4:6: "Be anxious for nothing, but in everything by prayer and supplication, with thanksgiving, let your requests be made known to God." Verse 7 continues by saying, "...and the peace of God, which surpasses all understanding, will guard your hearts and minds through Christ Jesus." *Anxious* here means "to be careful for." This is saying, "Don't be worried about anything." The word *nothing* includes everything you could possibly need—house, job, car, husband, wife, health, protection for your family, and so forth. In other words, Paul was writing that you should not have a single care, because you can make your request known to God.

There was a time when I would worry about everything. My first response to a problem was to worry about it. Until I discovered this formula, I would worry about my worries! In the natural world, therapists and psychologists who deal with people who are overly anxious will often have the person write down a list of those things he or she is most worried about. Then the therapist will advise that person to look at that list in a week or a month. It is amazing how many things that are at the top of your "worry list" today are absolutely irrelevant tomorrow or the day after.

However, if you worry enough, you will indeed have something on that list that won't go away—you will make yourself physically ill with worry. Doctors tell us that stress is a leading contributor to heart disease. People under stress have higher blood pressure and sometimes even other physical problems, such as hair falling out or skin lesions. Other people bite their fingernails or have other physical routines that are detrimental to their health—all because of *worry*. Jesus said in the Sermon on the Mount:

> Therefore I say to you, do not worry about your life, what you will eat or what you will drink; nor about your body, what you will put on. Is not life more than food and the body more than clothing? Look at the birds of the air, for they neither sow nor reap nor gather into barns; yet your heavenly Father feeds them. Are you not of more value than they? Which of you by worrying can add one cubit to his stature? So why do you worry about clothing? Consider the lilies of the field, how they grow: they neither toil nor spin; and yet I say to you that even Solomon in all his glory was not arrayed like one of these. Now if God so clothes the grass of the field,

which today is, and tomorrow is thrown into the oven, will He not much more clothe you, O you of little faith?

Therefore do not worry, saying, "What shall we eat?" or "What shall we drink?" or "What shall we wear?" For after all these things the Gentiles seek. For your heavenly Father knows that you need all these things. But seek first the kingdom of God and His righteousness, and all these things shall be added to you. Therefore do not worry about tomorrow, for tomorrow will worry about its own things. Sufficient for the day is its own trouble.

—MATTHEW 6:25–34

Much of this sounds like what we looked at earlier in Matthew 7:7–11, where Jesus said in verse 11: "If you then, being evil, know how to give good gifts to your children, how much more will your Father who is in heaven give good things to those who ask Him!" God knows what you need. Worrying about what you need won't change things one iota. *Praying* about them will, and that is why Paul said to let your requests be made known to God. He *knows them already*—that isn't the issue. Making them known to Him is part of the process by which you acknowledge that He is your source. In that long passage in Matthew, Jesus used the phrase, "Do not worry," or "Why do you worry?" no less than four times. How many times must the Son of God command you to do something before you obey? Matthew 6:33 is the key, when Jesus said to "seek first the kingdom of God, and all these *things* will be added to you" (emphasis added).

The antidote to worry is to speak
faith based on Scripture. If all you do
is walk around mumbling the same
ten verses all day long, at least that is
time not spent in unbelief or worry.

A lot of religious people have a problem with material things. They get upset if you drive a car that's too nice or if you wear clothes that are too expensive. Yet here we have Jesus the Christ saying that God would add things to you. If God didn't want you to have things, why in the world would Jesus Himself promise us "things" if we sought first the kingdom of God?

The whole point of Matthew 6:25–34 is not that you don't need things. Jesus Himself said that the heavenly Father knew you need things. He knows that if you have a job a long distance away from your home, you need some transportation! He knows that you cannot walk around naked. This is where we constantly get hung up. God doesn't know price tags. He could care less if you have a $20 suit or a $2000 suit—*as long as you don't care.* By care, I mean, care to the point of worry.

Don't say, "I just can't help it! I just worry!" You are calling God a liar. He has provided a way for us not to worry. Look at Hebrews 13:15: "Therefore by Him let us continually offer the sacrifice of praise to God, that is, the fruit of our lips." Would you agree that the word *continually* means "all the time"? Without ceasing? Once again, it's impossible for you to

187

say one thing and think another. You think what you say. So the best technique, if you will, for overcoming worry is to get into a permanent state of praise flowing from your lips.

Notice that Paul didn't say you could *think* good thoughts about God, but rather you had to offer the sacrifice of praise from the fruit of your lips. Jesus, in Matthew 12:34, said, "For out of the abundance of the heart the mouth speaks." If you can't speak praise and thanksgiving to God, Jesus said there was nothing in your heart. And if it is in your heart and you are not saying it, you are disobedient to God. So which is it? The antidote to worry is to speak faith based on Scripture. If all you do is walk around mumbling the same ten verses all day long, at least that is time not spent in unbelief or worry.

## STEP 7: MAKE YOUR WORDS A STATEMENT OF FAITH

Ingredient seven is similar to the last two: make every word relative to what you've asked in prayer *a statement of faith* instead of a statement of unbelief. Once you have prayed a petition prayer—the prayer of faith—everything out of your mouth from that point forward must build up your faith, not tear it down. If you are ill and you go to the doctor and he says, "How is this medication working?" you cannot lie and say, "I feel fine," if you don't feel fine. But you can say, "Doctor, praise God that you've identified the problem, and I believe I'm healed, but in the meantime, let's address these symptoms with another medication, because I'm still under attack from some pain." It's all about the wording, and words are critical, for we have already seen that death and life are in the power of the tongue. You can convey whatever accurate information you need to, whether it is to a doctor, accountant, financial advisor, or lawyer, without drifting into statements of unbelief. You can tell your attorney, "I believe God has bailed me out of this situation, but until I see exactly how, we need to fight this lawsuit." Reframe everything in faith terms. It is not a lie to confess what God has *done* while addressing what you *still need to do*.

Related to this, people often have a problem with *feeling* like they have, or don't have, faith. "Isn't it lying," people have asked me, "if I say that I have faith, when I really don't feel like it?" If you phrase it like that, yes, indeed, it would be lying. But remember, "We walk by faith, not by sight [or "not by feelings"]." Having faith is not true because you feel it; it's true because it's true. Unless something is really wrong physically, you can't feel your brains, but you still have them.

---

## Talk God's words. Repeat His promises. Personalize His blessings to yourself.

---

One of the greatest breakthroughs I ever had was when I learned that your level of faith is not measured by your emotional response to issues. Some people can cry at a Wal-Mart opening. I know of a fellow who nearly bursts into tears just watching *The Lion King*. Feelings have nothing to do with faith! This has been one of the devil's greatest deceptions on the church, to confuse emotion with faith. You might be a person who never cries, or it might take a lot to get you to laugh out loud or shout for joy. We are all different. You are no more, or less, *spiritual* than someone who dances in the aisles or who blubbers like a baby every time they watch *Old Yeller*.

In Romans 12:3, Paul wrote: "For I say, through the grace given to me, to everyone who is among you, not to think of himself more highly than he ought to think, but to think soberly, as God has dealt to each one a measure of faith." (The King James says, "God hath dealt to every man the measure of faith," which tells us that we all start off the same. No one has more faith than anyone else.)

But you can get more faith for faith by *saying* it. It is just as easy to think positive thoughts about your faith as negative thoughts, especially if you keep in mind that *no* godly prayer request is unheard or unanswered. Remember that just because you don't have it now doesn't mean you won't get it very soon. One of the most important words for a faith believer is *yet*: "Lord, I haven't seen this *yet*, but I believe I have already received it, and it will be made manifest any minute." Talk God's words. Repeat His promises. Personalize His blessings to yourself. And once again, this requires that you know God's Word so you can say God's words. How can you think God's thoughts when you don't know what they are?

> What do you believe? Well, that's
> up to you, but if you want results,
> you better believe the Word.

Note that the verse says that we should not think more highly of ourselves than we "ought to think." That tells me I ought to think highly of myself. What is the proper balance, then? I submit to you that the proper thinking about yourself is to say what God says about you and to think what God thinks about you. If God cared enough to send His own Son to die for you, then you must be worth something.

Jesus told Peter in a vision about food, "What God has cleansed you must not call common." Other Bible translations interpret that phrase as, "What God has called clean, do not call unclean." This is about more than food, though—it is about you. Once you have been created a "new creature" in Christ Jesus, you are *not* an "old sinner saved by grace." Not anymore! You *were*, but that's not you now. You are a new creature in Jesus, a brother of the Messiah, and a son of the most high God. Exactly how highly *should* you think of yourself, then?

That's why Paul says in Hebrews 10:23, "Let us hold fast the confession of our hope without wavering, for He who promised is faithful." The King James says, "Let us hold fast the confession of our faith." That word *confession* is also translated "profession," as in "Let us hold fast our profession of our faith." Either way, you are holding on to—clinging to, professing—the confession of what you believe. What do you believe? Well, that's up to you, but if you want results, you better believe the Word.

## REVIEWING THE STEPS

In review, these are the steps we have covered in the formula for an answered petition prayer:

1. Determine what you want, and find scriptures that promise you that.

2. Ask the Father, in Jesus's name, for what you want, believing you receive it when you ask.

3. Let every thought and desire affirm that you have what you asked for.

4. Guard against every evil thought that comes into your mind, and watch closely your associations and observations.

5. Think constantly on the promises on which you base the answer to your prayer.

6. Think on the love, mercy, goodness, and blessings of God to boost your faith.

7. Make every word relative to what you've asked in prayer a statement of faith instead of a statement of unbelief.

When you master these ingredients, you will begin to see prayers answered every time, and always with a *yes* and *amen*.

# Reflections From "Affirming Your Answered Prayer"

# Reflections From "Affirming
Your Answered Prayer"

# CHAPTER SEVEN

# A MODEL PRAYER

*Lift up your face to God.*
*You will make your prayer to Him,*
*He will hear you....*
*You will also declare a thing,*
*And it will be established for you;*
*So light will shine on your ways.*
*—Job 22:26–29*

I have described six different types of prayer in the earlier chapters and have given you seven important steps for receiving answers to your petition prayers. Understanding that, you may be wondering what a "typical" prayer looks—and sounds—like. Before I outline for you a "typical" prayer a believer might pray, I can tell you my personal prayer habit. I pray about an hour a day—twenty to thirty minutes in English, and the remainder of the time in the Spirit. This costs me, as I have to rise early to work in an hour of prayer before I start my day, but I find that if I do not pray, first thing, every day, I pay for it later. Are you willing to pay what it will cost to have your prayers answered, every time?

Once you make the decision to dedicate a regular part of your life to prayer, you then have to create the time, because you can bet the devil will not allow you to "work it in." Prayer is not something that you should just *fit* into your schedule: it is the key factor that allows the rest of your schedule to function. There is not a professional ball team in America, whether it's football, baseball, or basketball, that does not warm up before starting a practice or the game. Couldn't they get more practice time in if they got rid of that twenty minutes of warm-ups first? Of course, but the result would be more injuries—*more serious* injuries. If you approach your prayer time as optional, as something to be squeezed in, then soon you will not be praying at all. Some people I know pray in the shower, which can run up a water bill, but if that's what you have to do to get away from distractions, so be it. Others pray in the Spirit in their cars. That's fine, but if you try that in English, your attention will be divided, and you'll either mess up your prayer or have an accident. I prefer praying the first thing in the morning, because it sets the tone for the whole day. Then I never get into a situation where I say, "Uh oh, I should have prayed about that!" No, the Spirit will take care of those situations.

Remember also that the devil will do his best to distract you. You will have phone calls, pet "emergencies," family interruptions, even physical discomfort or itching—anything to get you off schedule. And if the devil can get you off schedule once or twice, pretty soon he can get you off schedule every day.

## Is There a Model for Prayer I Can Use?

I'm sure you want a model or *prototype* prayer. Some people lack confidence in developing their own prayers. With a little practice you will gain confidence, but let me start you off with some suggestions.

In his prayer for Gaius, John prayed this way: "I pray that you may prosper in all things, and be in health, just as your soul prospers" (3 John 2). John's prayer is a laundry list, if you will, of what John had *already prayed for* in Gaius's case. He was telling Gaius, "Brother, in the past we've set ourselves in agreement on these things, and I just want to let you know I'm keeping up my end of the bargain." I believe that from John's words we can assume that John had included these things in his prayer time.

Let me suggest one simple prayer of faith that you could plug into anyone's life situation.

### 1. Begin with thanksgiving.

*Heavenly Father, thank You so much for all Your blessings, and for all Your gifts…*

Here you might want to list the things you are thankful for—good health, a job, a nice house, a wonderful spouse or children. Whatever it is, thank God for it. Don't be in a hurry. This might take some time.

## 2. Confess your faith in God and His Son.

*Father, I'm a believer and not a doubter. Jesus is
Lord. I believe in my heart that He has been raised
from the dead. And I give thanksgiving that I am
born again. I'm a believer and not a doubter. Thank
You, Jesus, for Your sacrifice and that You lived a perfect life, died on the cross for me, rose from the grave
for me, defeated hell and death for me, and sit at the
right hand of the Father making intercession for me.
Praise You, Jesus!*

Don't be in a rush. You can never go wrong by praising
God and His Son.

## 3. Pray for those in authority over you.

In 1 Timothy 2:1–2, Paul tells us that we should pray for
our leaders.

Therefore I exhort first of all that supplications, prayers,
intercessions, and giving of thanks be made for all men,
for kings and all who are in authority, that we may lead
a quiet and peaceable life in all godliness and reverence.

Paul was saying that we need to pray for all men to come
into the knowledge of salvation, to give thanks, and to intercede for all those in authority over us. This is for *our* benefit,
not theirs, so that we may lead peaceful lives. You can't have
a very good prayer life if you are worried about rival gangs
breaking down your doors.

During my prayer time I thank God for the president, whoever he is, the vice president, the members of the House and Senate, the Supreme Court, our governor, our mayor, and the police, judges, and fire personnel over me, that I may live in peace. Just imagine what an incredibly peaceful world it would be if every one of those people were born-again Christians! And this is the wonderful part: even when the *king*, as it were—the president or the governor or whoever—is not a believer, God can use that person.

In the Bible, God constantly directed the kings of Babylon and other countries to show favor to the Jews living under their authority. Some of that was due to the prayer intercessions of the priests and prophets. There will be times when you pray for someone in authority over you and say, "I can't believe they just voted that way," or "I can't believe she just made that speech, it's so out of character." But that's God at work. If you don't pray for these people—especially the nonbelievers—you are just handing them over to the devil.

Remember, not all believers have it as well as you do! Bind the demonic spirits that are attacking Christians through governments, and loose the protective angels that they might keep believers safe and free.

At some point, you should pray for the holy church and all believers. Pray for the Christians battling repressive governments—men and women who literally take their lives in their hands by worshiping God. Pray that we come into a "unity of the faith" and that God's people stop bickering among themselves so they can work together to accelerate the spreading of the gospel. Thank God for ministers, pastors, teachers, prophets, and evangelists. I name the people I know who are in ministry and specifically ask God to bless them, and I set myself in agreement with them that their needs are met.

## 4. Pray for revelation knowledge.

Paul also said we should pray for revelation knowledge. Pray for greater spiritual understanding, and pray that believers around the world are protected and that they may exercise their faith in peace. Pray for the spread of the gospel, that with the harvest ready, laborers are coming forth. In that vein, it's appropriate to pray that government barriers against Christianity are lifted, whether in communist countries or in Muslim countries where Christians are, to this day, enslaved. Remember, not all believers have it as well as you do! Bind the demonic spirits that are attacking Christians through governments, and loose the protective angels that they might keep believers safe and free.

## 5. Add your personal confession about your need.

When you are ready, next move to your personal confession about your needs and your circumstances.

*Father, I believe that the things You have promised me in Your Word belong to me. I intend to know what they are. Satan, I rebuke you in the name of Jesus! Take your hands off my body. Take your hands off my home. Take your hands off my finances. Take your hands off my children and my family, and get out of my affairs. The blood of the Lamb is over me. I belong to God. You, Satan, are not my Lord. Jesus is Lord, and He has defeated you permanently to reclaim the world and to reclaim me. I don't have to do what you say, devil. I don't have to receive what you give. I believe I am healed from the tip of my toes to the top of my head. I believe through His stripes I was healed, and since I was healed, I am healed. Jesus is the champion of my salvation, the giver of my healing, and the author of my faith. God is Jehovah Rapha, the "God who heals me," and I receive that healing.*

If you have a particular medical challenge, put it in! Pray specifically over that issue. Otherwise, you can just thank God that you have a healthy heart, arteries, lungs, bronchial tubes, stomach, esophagus, liver, and so on. When I pray, I name every part of my body I can think of, thanking God they are healthy. That's *playing offense* over those parts of your body that might be attacked. You are putting up a faith shield around them. Playing *defense* involves praying over any part of your body that is already under attack, and you know what they say: "The best defense is a good offense."

Quote Psalm 91, and make it personal:

*I am not afraid of the terror by night, nor the arrow that flies by day, nor the pestilence that walks in darkness, nor the destruction at noonday. Father, Your Word promises that even though a thousand fall at my side, and ten thousand at my right hand, it shall not come near me, nor shall any evil befall me, nor shall any plague come near my dwelling, because You have given Your angels charge over me. Once again, loose Your angels that they might protect me. I bind demonic spirits that they will have no place in my body, my family, or my home.*

Now begin confessing protection over your family.

*Father, Your Word promised that my seed would be blessed, and that if I raised a child up in the way he should go, he would never depart. Lord, I've tried to put You in front of my family at all times. I thank You for my family. Protect them. I pray the blood of Jesus over them as they go about their lives today. Keep them safe. Reveal Yourself to them.*

## 6. Pray for your enemies.

If you are a normal, average person, you will have some enemies. Confess what Deuteronomy said—that they would come at you one way and go away fleeing seven. Jesus said to pray for specific enemies. Pray for their conversion, if they are not Christians, and pray for their eyes to be opened to their behavior if they are. Confess in line with the Word that you will add patience to your love when you deal with them.

---

Wherever you pray, be sure to set aside someplace where you won't be interrupted. Remember that one of the devil's best tricks is distraction.

---

We also have enemies in the world that want to kill us. Paul tells us in Romans that we have a police force and an army to "execute wrath," not merely to dispense justice. There is a reason for this. If you do not want people to engage in Mafia-style vendettas, each seeking his own revenge, you must be assured that the government (which you prayed for above) will take care of threats to our nation and our neighborhoods. So we are well within our godly rights to pray that God deliver our enemies into our hands as a nation. You might not be comfortable with that, but I have no problem thanking God that He has already delivered our enemies into our hands, including leaders in al Qaeda and other terrorist movements. Of course, if you want to pray for their conversions, do that too, and if they get converted before getting captured, so much the better.

Here is an amazing thing: Proverbs says that when you do good to your enemies, for example, praying for them, you "will heap coals of fire on his head" (Prov. 25:22). Have you ever sincerely (not facetiously) said to a genuine enemy, "I'll pray for you," and watched what happens? That person will usually react like you threw hot fire on him or her and may say indignantly: "How dare you think I need *you* to pray for *me*."

Look at Proverbs 24:17–18:

> Do not rejoice when your enemy falls,
> And do not let your heart be glad when he stumbles;
> Lest the LORD see it, and it displease Him,
> And He turn away His wrath from him.

So this is really tricky. When you pray for your enemies, you really are heaping burning coals on their heads. It *is* going to cause them discomfort—but if you take pleasure in that, you will actually interfere with God's dealing with that person!

### 7. Pray for your financial and material needs.

Having prayed for those in authority over you, your health, your family, next address your financial and material needs.

> *Father, I believe my needs are met. The Son has made me free! I am free from need. Your Word says that You loved us more than the birds of the air or the lilies of the field, more than human fathers—who give their children good gifts—love their kids. So my needs are met according to Your riches in glory. I am redeemed from the curse. The blessing of Abraham is mine. I'm blessed coming in, blessed going out, above and not beneath, the head and not the tail, blessed in the city, and blessed in the field. I'm a victorious overcoming conqueror and more than a conqueror.*

Any other confessions or promises from the Word related to material things that you find, you can put in this section. If you have a need in this area, this is where you state it. Some people work on computers all day, and for them to get their work done, they need their computers to function. Pray over those computers. Other people are truck drivers or operate machinery. Pray over those devices. And I would never get on an airplane without praying over that aircraft and the pilot and crew, that they be blessed in the name of Jesus and that I have a safe trip to where I'm going. Other people will be cursing that plane, especially if it's late, so you better be blessing it!

> *Father, thank You for my car. I need a new car, Father. This one has carried me many miles, but I need one that burns less oil and is safer and more fuel efficient.* [Or if you just want a new car, you don't need a reason!] *I want a Mercedes, Lord, because I like them. I want to drive one. Thank You, Father, for meeting this desire of my heart. I've put You first in all ways, Father, that I can think of. Your Word said if I did that, all these things would be added unto me. So Father, thank You for Your promise. I believe I have already received it, and I thank You for that new car.*

Once you've addressed physical, job, and material needs, address any specific family situation or job situation or anything troubling your spirit.

## 8. Conclude your prayer by praying in the Spirit.

At that point, I close my prayer in English and spend time praying (interceding) in the Holy Spirit. That way, I've covered all my bases. I know that there is not one issue that I should have addressed but didn't, and not one request that I should have made but forgot. There is not one time that I finish praying in the Spirit that I am not satisfied that everything that needed to be said, by me to God and by God to me, was said.

The most important ingredient for answered prayer, of course, is to pray. You can't get practice at praying until you start to pray. The writer William F. Buckley, who at his peak would write a newspaper column every day, edit a magazine, and turn out two novels a year, was once asked how he wrote so much. Buckley said, "I get up in the morning, brush my teeth, then sit down and start to type." Prayer is the same process. Some people have a prayer closet, some have a prayer room, or some pray in bed. Wherever you pray, be sure to set aside someplace where you won't be interrupted. Remember that one of the devil's best tricks is distraction. But most of all, find a *regular time* to pray. No matter what, nothing must come between you and that prayer time.

Begin today. Begin right now. Start immediately finding out God's promises for you, and begin listing what He has already done. You will notice a change in your life, and I can assure you that you too can say with confidence, "God hears my prayers and answers them all."

# Reflections From "A Model Prayer"

# Reflections From "A Model Prayer"

_____

_____

_____

_____

_____

_____

_____

_____

_____

_____

_____

_____

_____

_____

_____

_____

# About the Author

Apostle Frederick K. C. Price was the founder and pastor of Crenshaw Christian Center in Los Angeles, California, and Crenshaw Christian Center East in Manhattan, New York. He was known worldwide as a teacher of the biblical principles of faith, healing, prosperity, and the Holy Spirit. During his more than sixty-five years in ministry, countless lives were changed by his dynamic and insightful teachings that truly "tell it like it is."

His television program, *Ever Increasing Faith Ministries* (*EIFM*), had been broadcast throughout the world for more than forty-three years and currently airs in many of the largest markets in America, reaching an audience of millions of households each week. *EIFM* is also webcast on the Internet via www.faithdome.org. The *EIFM* radio program is heard on stations across the world, including the continent of Europe via shortwave radio.

The author of more than fifty popular books teaching practical application of biblical principles, Apostle Price pastored one of America's largest church congregations, with a membership of approximately twenty-two thousand. The Los Angeles church sanctuary, the FaithDome, is among the most notable and largest in the nation, with a seating capacity of more than ten thousand.

In 1990 Apostle Price founded the Fellowship of Inner-City Word of Faith Ministries (FICWFM), which later became the Fellowship of International Christian Word of Faith Ministries before disbanding in 2017. Members of FICWFM included more than three hundred churches from all over the United States and various countries. The Fellowship, which met regionally throughout the year and hosted an annual convention, was not a denomination. Its mission was to provide fellowship, leadership, guidance, and a spiritual covering for those desiring a standard of excellence in ministry.

Apostle Price held an honorary doctor of divinity degree from Oral Roberts University and an honorary diploma from Rhema Bible Training Center.

He departed this life on February 12, 2021.

For more information, to receive a catalog, or to be placed on the EIF mailing list, please contact:

Crenshaw Christian Center
PO Box 90000
Los Angeles, CA 90009
Phone: 800-927-3436

Check your local TV or webcast listing for *Ever Increasing Faith Ministries,* or visit our website at www.faithdome.org.

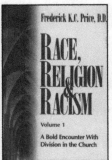

## *How Faith Works:*
### Special Edition

The principles of faith are God's design to bring you everything you will ever need in the earth realm. If you are wondering why some Christians have greater results with the Word of God than others, then you need to read this teaching on how to live by faith. Everything in the kingdom of God is activated by faith, so get this understanding and be empowered.

1-883798-78-7: Leather Bound
1-883798-57-4: Paperback

This teaching is also available on CD and cassette. For the latest information on other books and audio products, please contact us at:

**(800) 927-3436**
**Crenshaw Christian Center**
P. O. Box 90000 • Los Angeles, CA 90009 • www.faithdome.org